Listening
to Learn

Listening to Learn

Audiobooks
Supporting Literacy

Sharon Grover

Lizette D. Hannegan

AMERICAN LIBRARY ASSOCIATION

Chicago   2012

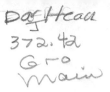
Sharon Grover is a longtime audiobook listener and reviewer. She has served on and chaired Selected Audiobooks for Young Adults (now called Amazing Audiobooks for Young Adults), served on the inaugural Odyssey Award Committee, and chaired the 2010 Odyssey Award Committee. Currently, she is head of the Youth Services Department at the Hedberg Public Library in Janesville, Wisconsin, where she shares favorite audiobook titles with her young patrons. Fifteen years at the Arlington (Virginia) Public Library allowed her the good fortune to work with her friend and colleague Liz Hannegan, as well as a host of amazing middle school readers and listeners. Sharon has written articles and columns and presented workshops—many of them with Liz Hannegan—on using audiobooks to promote literacy. She is proud of turning Liz into an audiobook devotee and is happy to have become a curriculum junkie in return.

Lizette (Liz) Hannegan is now retired from the Arlington (Virginia) Public Schools, after working twenty-two years as an elementary and middle school librarian and as the district library media supervisor. Advocating for audiobooks has resulted in conference presentations, grants for the use of audiobooks in instructional settings, and journal and review articles. She has been an Audies judge, a 2010 Odyssey Award Committee member, and the 2012 Odyssey Award chair. Growing up in Baltimore, Maryland, she feels that the Enoch Pratt Free Library was a source for her love and support for libraries. She has used her bachelor's degree in English literature and master's degree in library science to demonstrate that libraries are the place where all young people begin their journey of listening and learning. For Liz, the best part of completing this book has been working with a kindred spirit, friend and colleague Sharon Grover.

© 2012 by the American Library Association. Any claim of copyright is subject to applicable limitations and exceptions, such as rights of fair use and library copying pursuant to Sections 107 and 108 of the U.S. Copyright Act. No copyright is claimed for content in the public domain, such as works of the U.S. government.

Printed in the United States of America

16 15 14 13 12   5 4 3 2 1

Extensive effort has gone into ensuring the reliability of the information in this book; however, the publisher makes no warranty, express or implied, with respect to the material contained herein.

ISBNs: 978-0-8389-1107-5 (paper); 978-0-8389-9394-1 (PDF); 978-0-8389-9395-8 (ePUB); 978-0-8389-9396-5 (Mobipocket); 978-0-8389-9397-2 (Kindle). For more information on digital formats, visit the ALA Store at alastore.ala.org and select eEditions.

Library of Congress Cataloging-in-Publication Data

Library of Congress Cataloging-in-Publication Data available at http://catalog.loc.gov/.

Cover design by Kirstin Krutsch. Book design in Learning Curve, Liberation Serif, and Helvetica Neue.

♾ This paper meets the requirements of ANSI/NISO Z39.48-1992 (Permanence of Paper).

To our husbands, Greg and K. P.,
who gave us steadfast interest and support,
have grown used to us being connected
to headphones and earbuds, and have become
avid and critical listeners too!
Thank you for your love and encouragement.

Contents

Contents

Preface

A working collaboration, a friendship, and an advocacy for audiobooks brought us together almost twenty years ago. The setting was a middle school library where young adolescents would come during their lunchtime for the Teen Advisory Board (TAB) book discussion. We—Sharon (the public librarian) and Liz (the school librarian)—worked together every two weeks as the sixth, seventh, and eighth graders came during their separate lunch periods. We discovered that we both enjoyed the students and talking about our devotion to children's and young adult literature. The increased availability of audiobooks became a topic not only with the students but also with us. Liz was a bit behind ("I can't possibly drive while listening to an audiobook!"), whereas Sharon quickly became an audiobook devotee. And then a mini-breakthrough occurred ("I *can* listen to audiobooks while driving!"), and both of us found ourselves talking and advocating for the use of audiobooks in many settings, especially classrooms and in reading assignments. We rely on each other's expertise, which comes from different library perspectives and experiences, and we have found a wonderful professional collaboration and a personal friendship. We have read and listened voraciously, written a number of professional articles, and presented at conferences and workshops on the topic that you are about to read. Welcome to *Listening to Learn: Audiobooks Supporting Literacy.*

Acknowledgments

We express our appreciation to educators, renowned authors, audiobook experts, and publishers for their contributions and comments. These quotes and contributions from them, which can be found throughout the text, reveal the increasingly broad use of audiobooks across disciplines, thus validating and enriching the central thesis of our work.

Without the support of many audiobook publishers who sent us new titles when we requested something specific for this book, many of the latest stories that you will read about would not have been available to us.

We also appreciate the guidance of our editor, Stephanie Zvirin, who has encouraged our work for years and has helped us bring this book to fruition.

1

How It All Begins

*T*hose of us who work with children and teens in school and public library settings appreciate the thrill of reading a great book. Curling up with a favorite author or genre brings enormous satisfaction to book people.

But for many of the students we serve, that love of reading and the satisfaction of a well-told story just doesn't happen. Because we want students to participate in rich literature experiences, and because we know how critical reading is to future success, we are always looking for ways to engage them with the written word. Current audiobook productions—with their high production values, stellar narrators, and wide variety of formats—can be one avenue to reach these reluctant or struggling readers, as well as their proficient peers who are looking for more time to include reading in their busy schedules.

The Search Institute has created the 40 Developmental Assets list, which pulls together "elements in human experience that have long-term, positive consequences for young people."[1] These assets are thought to predict success and encourage students to engage in fewer risky behaviors, particularly as they move into middle and high school. Among the forty assets are the external asset of positive support from nonfamily-member adults and the internal asset of reading for pleasure. A caring teacher or librarian armed with a list of exciting audiobooks can provide both of these things to students who don't read or to those who are reading, but rarely just for pleasure. Those of us who enjoy reading for pleasure, either with our eyes or with our ears, understand the importance of the diversion this experience provides.

Working with these students and their families also offers another opportunity for collaboration between schools and public libraries. Because public library materials budgets do not need to support textbooks and learning software, they are often able to include more audiobooks in their collections. Teachers and school librarians can form effective partnerships with their public library colleagues to make these materials available to students. Public librarians will be happy to see that collection circulate outside of vacation times and may even be willing to help booktalk titles in the classroom.

Katherine Kellgren, one of today's foremost narrators of audiobooks for children and teens, has recorded more than 125 audiobooks, including several Odyssey Honor titles. In 2009 Kellgren won the Audie Award for Best Solo Narration (Female), and in 2010 she was named one of *AudioFile* magazine's "Golden Voices." She eloquently described to us her experience of listening as a young person herself:

> I grew up listening to audiobooks, and they were vitally important to my development as a child as they made me curious to read for myself, in fact they really helped me to fall in love with literature. The first time I came into contact with a lot of my favorite authors, it was through the audio versions of their work. Listening opened up so many worlds to me in a way that was very intimate and seemed to speak directly to me. It made the work of great authors both in children's and adult literature seem less intimidating, and excited my curiosity to pick up books in print form. I sometimes hear the argument that if children listen to audiobooks it's somehow "cheating," that it's too easy and discourages them from reading for themselves. All I can say is that from my personal experience it has the exact opposite effect! That is one of the many reasons I feel so proud and so fortunate to be able to narrate books for children and young adults. It's my great hope that I can help contribute something to the lifelong adventure that begins when a child first [says,] "Read me a story."

The following chapters introduce some of the research linking audiobook listening and literacy development and equip readers with many titles, standards, and instructional activities to facilitate the use of audiobooks in classrooms, libraries, and homes. But first we'll take a look at how the audiobook business started and what we need to listen for to become critical listeners, selecting the very best for the young people in our lives.

The early days of audiobooks relied on LP recordings of available print material, with early rental programs to schools and public libraries.[2] In 1955, Anthony Ditlow, who was suffering from macular degeneration, founded Listening Library. Ditlow was familiar with audiobook productions for the blind and visually handicapped available from the Library of Congress, as well as the work of companies like Caedmon Audio and Spoken Arts.[3] In the 1960s, Lyndon Johnson's Great Society programs were pouring money into schools and public libraries, and Ditlow was positioned to move into children's books, taking advantage of the booming school market.[4] By focusing on the classic works that were staples of library and classroom collections, Ditlow "was pushing the educational value of audiobooks before the term *literacy* was used as it is today," according to his son, Tim Ditlow, vice president of Brilliance Audio.[5]

Early recordings were generally read by one person, with little or no embellishments—no character creations, no musical accompaniment, and no sound effects. Today's audiobooks are a far cry from those early days, with narrators now creating the voices of many characters or even with full-cast productions.

The most important aspect of selecting an audiobook is knowing whether the original text is something that will translate well to an aural medium. How does one choose among all those books out there the titles that will most engage listeners? Tim Ditlow, who grew up in the audiobook business at the company his parents, Anthony and Helen Ditlow, founded, had this to say to us:

> One of the most frequently asked questions of anyone involved in our business is, "How do you know which books to select for an audiobook production out of the thousands of titles published annually?"
>
> While many people wish a magic formula existed for predicting bestsellers, the fact remains that a publisher must be willing to take a gamble on what their intuition tells them is an outstanding novel.
>
> I believe chance favors the well-read publisher. By that I mean, if you really love a certain category, whether they be books for young adults, science fiction or romance novels, and if you read deeply in your field, over time you will get better at picking top sellers.
>
> For example, did I know a manuscript about a boy wizard would end up becoming the bestselling audiobook series in the history of the industry? No. Did I know it was a thoroughly engaging fantasy novel? Yes, but only because I had produced recordings by Lloyd Alexander, Susan Cooper, Madeleine L'Engle and Philip Pullman for the previous twenty years.

Speaking of producing, it helps if your editorial acumen is sharpened by having spent time in the studio. This way you can develop the "inner listening" wisdom to know which books will make great recordings.

Well, maybe there is a magic formula after all—read, read more and listen to your instincts!

Let's move on to what, exactly, we might be listening to in terms of the narration of an audiobook. Here is a sampling of different vocal interpretations (be sure to look at Mary Burkey's Audiobook Lexicon in appendix A for a more complete breakdown of what you're hearing on an audiobook).

First and foremost, we expect clarity and consistency in audio productions. The narrator should not sound as if he or she were reading from the bottom of a well. There should be no silent gaps between thoughts or chapters, and the sound quality or volume should not vary (in other words, the listener should not be able to tell when breaks were taken in the narrating process).

Pacing is a very important element in a narrator's tool kit. Too fast, and you can't understand what's being said. Too slow, and your attention wanders. Pacing should also be appropriate to the tenor of the story; it should move more quickly when there is exciting action and slow down for more contemplative scenes.

For audiobooks with one reader, here are a few ways the narration might be developed:

- A fully voiced narration, in which the narrator develops a distinct voice for each character
- A partially voiced narration, in which the reader develops a distinct voice for some characters but distinguishes others through pacing and inflection
- An unvoiced narration, in which pacing and inflection differentiate all the characters

Perhaps there is more than one reader. For example, there might be a male and a female narrator to differentiate genders, or there might be a full cast, with each member taking on an individual role in the book. In the case of full-cast recordings, attributives (e.g., "he said," "she said") are often removed from the text to produce a better narrative flow.

What about pronunciation? It should be clear, consistent, and correct. Proper names and place-names are particularly important. How many children knew how to pronounce the name of Harry Potter's friend Hermione before listening to the inimitable Jim Dale's excellent recordings of that iconic series?

In their article "Authentic Listening Experiences," Junko Yokota and Miriam Martinez state: "The audiobook narrator plays a role similar to that of a translator of a book from one language to another. A good translator can make a big difference in the reading experience through word choice and passage interpretation; likewise, the audiobook narrator helps mediate the story for the listener by selecting what tone to take, what types of voices to give to characters, what to emphasize, and how to engage the listener."[6]

With the increase in the publishing of multicultural books for children and teens, there has been a corresponding expansion of cultural diversity in audiobook production. Just as one always looks for cultural authenticity in the printed word, it is equally important to expect culturally accurate narration in an audiobook. This is true not only for cultures outside of the United States but also for cultures and localities within our borders. Just as the window to the wider world and the mirror to our children's own part of the world is important to us when purchasing and recommending print materials to our students, so is it vitally important when purchasing and recommending audiobooks. A narrator voicing a child from South Africa should employ the speech patterns, phrasing, and accents from that region. It is equally essential that a narrator voicing individuals from Wisconsin or West Virginia or South Boston be able to emulate the speech patterns, phrasing, and accents from those regions as well.

Now, more than ever, the careful listener must also consider music and sound effects when determining the effectiveness of an audiobook. Do these elements enhance the listening experience or detract from it? As Jo Carr so succinctly put it in her 1994 article on audiobook production, excellence is created by "respect for the original book, careful editing, technically superior recording, and inspired narration."[7]

Becoming a critical evaluator of audiobooks means listening and more listening—and still more listening. When new members are appointed each year to the Odyssey Award Committee, they are enjoined to carefully consider the award criteria before they begin their listening and as they continue listening throughout their year of service.[8] Reading reviews of audiobooks will also help in selecting the best for school, pleasure, and family listening; in chapter 10 you will find suggestions of journals in which you can find constructive reviews. Here, Sue-Ellen Beauregard, the media editor of *Booklist* magazine and consultant to the

Odyssey Award Committee, gave us some advice on what an audiobook review really is:

> Audiobook reviews are *not* book reviews and while that may sound like a simple concept, it means that audiobook reviews concentrate on the overall production values of the recording. I tell reviewers that the easy part of the process is listening to the audio and taking notes. The difficulty comes with writing a cogent critique of the audio, paying particular attention to the reader's (or readers') performance style, including voice quality, diction, timing, pacing, inflection, accents, tone, and method of distinguishing characters. In addition to critiquing the reader, reviewers must judge the overall technical qualities of the recording (sound, pauses, background music, sound effects). *Booklist* audio reviews provide librarians with credible interpretations of the audio recording and are never a review of the book. And although audio production has evolved over the past years with titles now including more author interviews and other special features, including PDF files and DVDs, the overall criteria for evaluating audios has remained much the same.

An Audio Publisher's Association survey conducted in the summer of 2010 discovered that there is "significant sharing" of audiobooks among friends and family.[9] Friends were, in fact, the major source of most audiobook suggestions among 27 percent of respondents, with websites coming in second, at 22 percent.[10] What you may find surprising is that a close third (21 percent) used librarians as their "leading source of recommendations."[11]

We take that as a sign to start listening and to find out what this audiobook and literacy revolution is all about!

NOTES

1. Search Institute, "Where the Asset Framework Comes From," http://www.search-institute.org/research/assets/background.
2. Biman Basu, "The Saga of Audiobooks," *Anil Aggrawal's Internet Journal of Book Reviews* 7, no. 2 (July–December 2008): 1, http://www.geradts.com/anil/br/index.html.
3. Shannon Maughan, "Sounds Like Celebration," *Publisher's Weekly*, March 7, 2005, 24–25.
4. Shawnee Smith, "Listening Library Outlasts Competition," *Billboard*, September 6, 1997, 85.
5. Maughan, "Sounds Like Celebration," 24–25.
6. Junko Yokota and Miriam Martinez, "Authentic Listening Experiences: Multicultural Audiobooks," *Book Links*, January 2004, p. 30.

7. Jo Carr, "Producing Audiobooks: How Do They Do It?" *Horn Book Magazine*, March–April 1994, p. 181.

8. Association for Library Service to Children, "ALSC/Booklist/YALSA Odyssey Award Eligibility and Criteria," www.ala.org/ala/mgrps/divs/alsc/ awardsgrants/bookmedia/odysseyaward/odysseyawardeligibilitycriteria/ odysseycriteria.cfm.

9. Jim Milliot, "Profiling Audiobook Customers," *Publisher's Weekly*, November 29, 2010, 4.

10. Ibid.

11. Ibid.

2

~

Why Listen?

People often ask, "Is listening to an audiobook cheating?" Our answer to that is a definite no! There are many proven literacy benefits to be gained from listening to a well-read audiobook, and we explore them in this chapter.

The process of reading is a complicated one. To be a fully successful reader, students must not only decode those often-incomprehensible marks on the page but also infer meaning from both literary and informational texts. For many students, this is a difficult task.

One of the most important developments for educational standards in the early twenty-first century has been the work of the Council of Chief State School Officers and the National Governors Association to create the national Common Core State Standards for English Language Arts and Literacy in History/Social Studies, Science, and Technical Subjects.[1] For the purposes of this discussion, hereafter, we refer to these standards as the Common Core.

The foundation behind the Common Core is to "ensure that all students are college and career ready in literacy no later than the end of high school." Research and evidence based, the Common Core is "aligned with college and work expectations" and draws on rigorous, international benchmarks to provide students with the tools to compete on a global playing field.[2]

The Common Core seeks to arm students with skills that will enable them to read, understand, and respond to increasingly complex texts, to acquire a wide-ranging vocabulary, to exploit technology and digital media appropriately, and to understand and appreciate other cultures and perspectives.

The Common Core also pays particular attention to instruction for English-language learners (ELLs), urging schools to provide language-rich environments that facilitate full participation in grade-level activities. The standards for ELLs also encourage modeling high-quality English language for students.

There has been a great deal of research supporting the use of audiobooks to promote vocabulary development, fluency, and comprehension. Because audiobooks remove the struggle to decode, Gene Wolfson, associate professor of education at Iona College, correctly notes that readers with special needs can gain skills in "recalling details, understanding sequence, making predictions, drawing conclusions, making inferences, and retelling," and that their more proficient peers can develop "skills and strategies in critical and creative thinking."[3]

In their seminal work *Becoming a Nation of Readers,* the Commission on Reading stated categorically, "The single most important activity for building the knowledge required for eventual success in reading is reading aloud to children."[4] Audiobooks can and do provide this critical activity in classrooms, automobiles, and homes across the country.

Avid readers who have regularly been read to are able to visualize a book's action in their minds, whereas aliterate students who have no recollection of being read to are unable to imagine text scenarios in their minds. These students rarely see reading as a "pleasurable or meaningful" experience.[5]

A successful strategy for motivating these students comes from a teacher in California who downloads audiobooks in her school's collection onto iPods that circulate to students who are, for a wide variety of reasons, reluctant readers. The iPods offer a "cool factor" in delivering a literature experience that allows for independent reading by increasing student motivation and confidence as well as providing access to difficult material. Students are encouraged to follow along in print editions while they listen so that "information [is] entering simultaneously through audio and visual channels."[6] Listening to literature gives students "the sense of the 'big picture' in a story rather than bogging them down with mechanics."[7]

Playaways are another popular delivery method for cool-factor listening (for a discussion of audiobook delivery formats, see chapter 10). An additional benefit to both iPods and Playaways is that they make the audiobook available for the entire class when the iPod or Playaway is plugged into portable speakers. This allows the classroom teacher to participate as a listener and to circulate through the classroom, assisting students who may need help focusing on the task at hand.

Preston Wilson, a high school English teacher in Auburn, New York, insists that "literature was never intended to be mediated by a fleet of English teachers . . . nor was it meant to be an anxious or laborious chore."[8] Audiobooks give struggling readers independence and allow them to enjoy the same literature experiences as their more proficient peers.

For ELLs, audiobooks are a particularly effective tool. Ten years ago, a remarkable collaboration was formed between the Berkeley Public Library and Berkeley High School in California. Dubbed "Earphone English," this effort to promote English-language learning through listening to audiobooks has grown to benefit hundreds of students over the years (see appendix C). From the early days when public librarian Francisca Goldsmith brought her audiobook review copies to teacher Heidi Ramirez Weber's classroom at lunchtime, the ELL students at Berkeley High School have listened to, discussed, and critiqued a wide variety of titles that would have been difficult to impossible for them to read on their own. This lunchtime club, which began with a handful of students, has expanded to include a website and a social network on Ning, both of which the students developed themselves. As Weber states, "You can see the lights go on in the eyes of the kids who can understand spoken English. They can now *get* the book."

Francisca Goldsmith, an instructor with Infopeople and a founder of Earphone English, provides a full update on the program in appendix C. Here is an important excerpt from the appendix that illuminates the benefits to the students and teachers (Heidi Ramirez Weber and Nancy Isaksen) who are part of Earphone English and sheds light on the value of school and public library collaboration:

■ Earphone English Club gives teens something that is in the present rather than seeming to be part of a great plan that will reward them in the future.

■ The club can be a place to share expertise with technology (e.g., the Ning designer's), crafts (paper folding and knitting have figured into some meetings), and other skills that fall outside the specifically literary and linguistic.

■ An annual trek to the public library for a movie and pizza celebration has demonstrated to library staff that the kids involved in the club have specific tastes in their movie choices, and these don't break along staff's expectations or assumptions. Among surprises have been the intense interest boys in the group had in *Twilight* and the high demand for a Holocaust film in another year.

■ Because Heidi [Ramirez Weber] was first introduced to *Speak* as an audiobook that several of her students discovered and loved, she placed it in the ninth-grade curriculum back in 2002.

■ Nancy [Isaksen] is an avid audiobook listener, while Heidi is not; Earphone English has encouraged them to discuss books between them in ways they hadn't explored earlier in their collaborations as teachers.

■ Student understanding of and commitment to the public library is built, often from the ground up, through the club, the meetings of which are regularly visited by public library staff. This experience has made such deep impressions on some that even years after high school graduation, they continue to be avid public library users.

For ELL students, listening to audiobooks improves not only vocabulary and comprehension but also their ability to communicate what they are reading with others. By acting as a scaffold that allows students to experience literature above their actual reading level, audiobooks encourage participation in class discussions with more proficient readers. Some teachers promote audiobook use in literature circles for this reason. All students, those who read well and those who do not, should be encouraged to voice their opinions, and audiobooks can definitely level the playing field.

Audiobooks offer an alternative reading delivery method to another at-risk group of students: boys. Studies show that boys lag behind girls in reading ability by as much as 10–15 percent, and they are not catching up.[9] Clearly, boys need help to motivate them to read. Jon Scieszka, author and 2008 Library of Congress Ambassador for Young People's Literature, tirelessly works to promote reading to boys. He told us: "In my Guys Read work, I've met all kinds of boys who are crazy for audiobooks. I think it's partially because audiobooks appeal to a lot of guys' love for messing around with any kind of technology. Guys also think they are getting away with something by listening instead of reading. We don't have to tell them that they are learning vocabulary, story structure, sentence composition, and a dozen other literacy skills."

According to Lisa Von Drasek, a librarian at the Bank Street College of Education, audiobooks can also serve as an effective classroom management tool. "One sixth-grade class who'd had trouble settling

down was now policing each other so as not to miss the latest install-
ment of Christopher Paul Curtis'[s] *Bud, Not Buddy.*"[10]

What about the audiobook experience for the avid readers who gob-
ble up books in our schools and libraries? For them, audiobooks provide
a means of extending their ability to read for pleasure and of forcing
them to slow down and fully grasp the language, humor, and context in
a work of literature. Listening to an audiobook means no skimming; for
better or for worse, listeners hear every word the author wrote, which
increases the literary connection for those speed readers.

For families, audiobooks offer a way to open discussion about seri-
ous topics. Although audiobooks for children and teens tend to circulate best during school vacation times, it really is a myth that children
(especially teens) do not commute. Think of the hours spent in the car
traveling to sports and other events that consume our family time. Kids
may keep quiet when they plug in to DVDs, portable gaming devices,
and MP3 players, but parents are missing out on a great opportunity to
have a shared literature experience that can lead to some meaningful
conversation with their children. Especially for parents of teens, this
opportunity is not one to miss.

Bruce Coville, the author of more than ninety books for children
and young teens and founder of Full Cast Audio, offered up the following observations on the benefits of shared family listening experiences:

> The first time I saw an SUV with television monitors in the back, my heart
> sank. Here was one more wedge being driven between parents and their
> children. In recent years the family car had become the last place many
> parents spent time alone with their kids. Now, with the arrival of in-auto
> DVD players we've given up even that ground and I think it's a tragic
> loss. When parents and children listen to an audiobook together they have
> a shared experience, something to talk about, think about, *feel* about. It
> can be a wonderful bonding experience, giving the parent a chance to talk
> about ideas and values at the same time that it increases an understanding
> of story and a love for books. But when the children are in the back seat,
> passively watching yet more TV, the car becomes one more place where
> we are *not* connecting with our children. Sharing an audiobook in the car
> brings parents and children closer in a way that they need, and that simply
> cannot happen when they are watching cartoons in isolation.

Families who homeschool children, and so do not participate in traditional school classrooms, also find audiobooks an effective means of
promoting reading and literacy. In the spring of 2011, we met Michelle

Hoffland, the mother of three boys, seven, eleven, and fourteen years old. She recalls that when one of the boys was younger, his attention span was shorter, but he was able to focus on reading by following along in the book while he was listening. She likes listening to audiobooks as a family because doing so includes everyone. One example she gave was when the family listened to *The Magician's Nephew*, by C. S. Lewis. Everyone enjoyed the experience, including the second grader, who could never have read the book independently. She states that listening to audiobooks has significantly improved the boys' vocabulary.

When the Hofflands listen to audiobooks as a family, they often pause and discuss aspects of the book, such as a different time period and how people lived in that period. For family listening, Michelle likes to choose older titles, feeling that the boys will "pick up the flashy new stuff themselves." They listen to a lot of historical fiction, such as *Where the Red Fern Grows*, by Wilson Rawls, and *Island of the Blue Dolphins*, by Scott O'Dell, which she says the boys would never have selected themselves because it's about a girl. The Hoffland family does much of their listening together on long car trips, at home on rainy days, or during the winter.

Eighth grader Isaiah and fifth grader Sam both are drawn to science fiction and action when making their own selections of audiobooks. They don't listen to books for schoolwork (although their mother clearly uses family listening time for instructional purposes), but they often listen for pleasure. Isaiah says he chooses the "really thick stuff" for audiobook listening and best likes narrators who "make it sound real." Isaiah and Sam both like listening because they can "multitask"—cleaning their room, playing games on their iPod, or "surfing the Net."

Sam likes narrators who "do the voices, screams, and sound effects" and often likes to read along while he's listening so he knows "how it's supposed to sound." Both boys say they listen before bed and always on long car trips. They get most of their audiobooks from the library, but they rip the CDs to their computer and then put them on their iPods. They wanted us to be sure to note that they always delete the books from their computers and iPods once they're finished listening to them. They're very honest fellows.

Isaiah very much enjoys Sync YA Listening, a summer listening program provided through *AudioFile* magazine (see chapter 8). The first year, he downloaded almost everything, and his favorite title of the summer was *The Lottery*, by Shirley Jackson. Sam, who listened along with Isaiah, was also very taken with *The Lottery*—a book neither boy would have selected on his own.

Now you know the answer to the question, "Why listen?" Audiobooks enhance literacy skills by building vocabulary, expanding comprehension capabilities, encouraging independence, and providing models for fluent reading. The following chapters focus on putting it all together with instructional standards and audiobook titles that showcase the rich variety of listening experiences available to promote reading for all the students we serve.

NOTES

1. For more information on the Common Core, visit the website of the Common Core State Standards Initiative (www.corestandards.org).
2. Common Core State Standards for English Language Arts and Literacy in History/Social Studies, Science, and Technical Subjects (www.corestandards .org/the-standards/english-language-arts-standards).
3. Gene Wolfson, "Using Audiobooks to Meet the Needs of Adolescent Readers," *American Secondary Education*, Spring 2008, 105–117.
4. Richard C. Anderson, Elfrieda H. Hiebert, Judith A. Scott, and Ian G. Wilkinson, with contributions from members of the Commission on Reading, *Becoming a Nation of Readers: A Report of the Commission on Reading* (Washington, D.C.: U.S. Department of Education, 1985), 23.
5. Kylene Beers, "Listen While You Read: Struggling Readers and Audiobooks," *School Library Journal*, April 1998, 30–35.
6. Linda Bomar, "iPods as Reading Tools," *Principal*, May–June 2006, 52–53.
7. Ibid.
8. Pamela Varley, "As Good as Reading? Kids and the Audiobook Revolution," *Horn Book Magazine*, May–June 2002, 251–262.
9. Ron Claiborne and Hanna Siegel, "New Study Shows Boys Lagging behind Girls in Reading," http://abcnews.go.com/WN/ study-shows-boys-lagging-girls-reading/story?id=10128586&page=1.
10. Lisa Von Drasek, "Heard Any Good Books Lately?" *Teaching Pre K–8*, May 2004, 90–91.

3
~

Audiobooks and Learning Standards

$\mathcal{A}$s indicated in the previous chapter, research supports the use of audiobooks to strengthen literacy skills. In selecting audiobooks as an instructional enhancement, numerous local, state, and national standards have been studied to demonstrate how audiobooks can serve as an effective tool. It has been observed that all curriculum subjects—language arts, social studies, science, mathematics, fine arts, foreign language—can connect with audiobook listening, and audiobook topics can integrate with many curriculum themes. From that foundation, the next thread to explore is learning standards and frameworks. This chapter presents and organizes some of the most relevant information and access points for local, state, and national instructional standards. We have found that the research presents a strong premise for how using audiobooks in classroom and library settings is an effective instructional tool. The discussion features various resources that provide a rationale for connecting audiobook themes with a wide range of standards, thus demonstrating that all good stories and information resources can be enhanced with listening experiences that become learning experiences.

STANDARDS AND EDUCATIONAL REFORM RESOURCES

The terminology for educational standards can be daunting—assessment and accountability, subject targets and themes, learning strands, curriculum mapping—the list seems endless. The path to best practices in student learning leads to exploring the instructional continuum. Teaching staff can connect and integrate regular classroom and library lessons with curriculum standards, especially when considering audiobooks and their inherent link to reading, no matter what the subject might be.

I not only require that my teacher-librarian students listen to an audiobook for their classes in children's and YA literature, I encourage them to locate audio versions of some of the other required books. My objective, of course, is to get them listening critically (with what we called our "Odyssey ears" on that first committee) to audiobooks. What they also discover is the joy of audio which serves for them as almost a one-on-one read-aloud session. They come to understand that audiobooks can assist struggling readers in their comprehension, can assist English Language Learners (ELL) with fluency, can introduce a classic to new readers, and can provide *time* to read for all of us who are often looking for a chance to curl up with a good book. I hope that these new teachers-librarians will then develop audiobooks as part of any collection they supervise, be it in the classroom, the school, or the community.

—Dr. Teri Lesesne, professor, Department of Library Science, Sam Houston State University, and member of the 2008 Inaugural Odyssey Award Committee

In our work we have found it interesting to compare various learning frameworks to determine whether they are similar in targeting subject- and grade-level objectives. Teachers have many avenues to bring together concrete examples of instructional themes and standards, from local curriculum departments, state education agencies, and national associations. Many large school systems provide such guidance, and smaller and/or rural areas often rely on state and national examples. One thing that does fluctuate is what is taught at what grade level across the country. A specific subject may be targeted in grade 3 in one state and in grade 5 in another—there do not seem to be distinct recommendations of what to teach when, except for the designation of elementary, middle/intermediate, and high school. As an example, ancient Greek and Roman history is introduced from grade 2 through grade 4, depending on the state and district.

Consequently, teachers, librarians, and parents will find it beneficial to choose several access points to discover which resources work best for their educational needs. A cautionary note: Finding an online path to locate specific learning standards is, at times, challenging because it requires multiple clicks and links to actually get to the standards. An important tip for researching standards is to always look at the "last updated" date at the bottom of any website. Some web pages have not been updated for several years, and information might not be current or accurate. We hope that what we provide here will ease the search for resources and learning guidelines and how they integrate with using audiobooks. We reference national, local, and state standards, as well as the most prominent subject associations and educational reform principles. The following resources can be used to provide background information that supports instructional practice.

Common Core State Standards Initiative

As discussed in chapter 2, the Common Core State Standards Initiative (www.corestandards.org) is an important national effort to provide consistent learning guidelines and a pathway for K–12 instructional targets that represent shared goals for the nation's students. The majority of states and the District of Columbia have formally adopted the Common Core. For this reason, many audiobook titles that we present in the following chapters are highlighted with subject- and grade-level goals that align with the Common Core and support the use of audiobooks for teaching and learning. Most of the examples that we cite focus on the English Language Arts Standards in the areas of literature and reading, even though the Common Core specifies "Standards for English Language Arts and Literacy in History/Social Studies, Science, and Technical Subjects."

The English Language Arts Standards are organized along the continuum from kindergarten through grade 12, with layers and strands that feature goals for students to be prepared for college and career. Introductory information to the content standards states what the Common Core does not cover, such as the lack of specificity for ELL students and students with special needs, and makes the proviso that the Common Core leaves much to educators for the design of the curriculum. The standards also recognize the broad range of student abilities, which make it difficult to create a one-size-fits-all environment for learning. The document calls for an integrated and interdisciplinary approach to instruction.

A strength of the English Language Arts Standards is the consistent presentation pattern. From kindergarten through grade 5, the Reading Standards include the following main concepts, which appear as section titles and run throughout the Standards: "Key Ideas and Details," "Craft and Structure," "Integration of Knowledge and Ideas," "Range of Reading and Level of Text Complexity." The categories within the Reading Standards section include the following:

- Reading: Literature
- Reading: Informational Text
- Reading: Foundational Skills (e.g., skills and processes such as phonics and fluency)
- Writing
- Speaking and Listening
- Language (e.g., conventions of standard English, knowledge of language, vocabulary, spelling, grammar)

Following the K–5 English Language Arts Standards, the Common Core provides charts and tables listing text exemplars for use in those grade levels. The full list of text exemplars, including excerpts from suggested literature, is located in appendix B of the Common Core State Standards, which displays extensive grade-level examples of literature to use with students. Throughout the chapters in this book that provide annotations for specific audiobooks, we have noted a number of Common Core text exemplars.

The Common Core recognizes that there is generally a single classroom teacher for kindergarten through grade 5, whereas grades 6 through 12 distinguish content subjects such as science, social studies and history, and technical subjects. Those subject standards were developed for these secondary grade levels. Therefore, the English Language Arts Standards for grades 6–12 contain the same format as for grades K–5, with a few minor changes. There are no foundational skills at the secondary level; grades 6, 7, and 8 are represented individually; and grades 9–10 and 11–12 are banded together. Again, text exemplars are briefly listed after the standards (see appendix B of the Common Core Standards). As each grade level progresses, the scaffolding for student goals builds on those of each prior grade.

The Reading Standards for Literacy in History/Social Studies, Science, and Technical Subjects for grades 6–12 include the same sections: "Key Ideas and Details," "Craft and Structure," "Integration of Knowledge and Ideas," "Range of Reading," and "Level of Text Complexity."

The History/Social Studies Standards concentrate on topic-related skills, such as reading primary sources and evaluating multiple sources for information. The Science and Technical Subjects Standards focus on experiment evaluation and analysis of technical text. Complementing the English Language Arts Standards, the Writing Standards within the History/Social Studies Standards center on writing reports related to historical events; the Writing Standards within the Science and Technical Subjects Standards cover science experiments and hypotheses.

The Literacy in History/Social Studies, Science, and Technical Subjects Standards are abbreviated in relation to the detailed English Language Arts Standards but give guidance for incorporating and integrating them into the curriculum, as do the English Language Arts Standards.

COMMON CORE STATE STANDARDS FOR MATHEMATICS

The companion to the Common Core Standards for English Language Arts and Literacy in History/Social Studies, Science, and Technical Subjects is the Common Core Standards for Mathematics (www.core stadards.org/the-standards/mathematics). The structure and presentation of the Mathematics Standards aligns with that of the English Language Arts Standards but naturally differs in content and perspective.

The Mathematics Standards are organized from kindergarten through grade 8 by grade level and then high school for specific math subjects such as algebra, geometry, and probability. The standards themselves clearly define what students should know and be able to do in mathematics. The progression begins in kindergarten with recognizing shapes and cardinal numbers and continues through the grades in a scaffold form that becomes more advanced and precise. Teachers receive detailed guidance for what student skills need to be achieved at each grade level.

For the purposes of this narrative, we give audiobooks that feature math concepts a range of grades (K–2, 3–5, 6–8, 9–12) and then suggest the type of math skill supported through the audiobook, such as number operations, proportion, and division.

As stated already, the majority of states have adopted the Common Core State Standards, but most have also created transition documents, crosswalks between the two, and are reviewing and revising their standards to align with or complement the Common Core. The full standards are available online so that all teachers, parents, librarians, and educators can follow the progression of learning expectations from kindergarten through grade 12.

When designing instructional lessons or units, the Common Core State Standards offer a national perspective for student achievement across the curriculum. And all curriculum subjects can be tied to the audiobooks featured in the upcoming chapters.

National Subject Area Professional Associations

Most curricular subject areas have a professional association that offers resources, professional development, and ongoing support for educators of that subject. The associations offer lessons, unit plans, ideas for long-term projects, conference workshops, and guidance on curriculum standards to their constituents. In the following section, we present an overview of these core curriculum associations.

NATIONAL COUNCIL OF TEACHERS OF ENGLISH

The National Council of Teachers of English (NCTE; www.ncte.org) publishes professional books that give educators, classroom teachers, reading specialists, librarians, and others specific materials to keep current with educational reform and trends in the field of language arts and literacy. The association's website also offers information and materials that provide links to lessons, professional development opportunities, and other subject-related topics.

The NCTE's publication *Standards for the English Language Arts*, in collaboration with the International Reading Association, gives teaching professionals substantial guidance on the subject. The English Language Arts Standards are concentrated around twelve statements that, paraphrased, feature some of the following goals:

- Students will read a wide range of fiction and nonfiction in many genres to gain understanding of their world and the human experience.
- Students will be able to analyze, interpret, and evaluate what they read.
- Students will be able to communicate in verbal and written form using their knowledge of language conventions.
- Students use various print and technology resources to complete research, evaluate data, and communicate their findings.
- Non-English-speaking students will use their first language to develop competency in the English language arts.
- Students will be able to use spoken, written, and visual language for learning, enjoyment, and to share information.

For the purpose of integrating the NCTE English Language Arts Standards with audiobook themes, it should be noted that the full standards are available online (www.ncte.org/standards). The strands of literature and literacy correlate with the inherent oral tradition that audiobooks represent, and the listings of grade-level titles in the following chapters demonstrate the connection between reading skills.

NATIONAL COUNCIL FOR THE SOCIAL STUDIES

Social studies offers many opportunities to connect audiobook use with instruction, including historical fiction, biography, and informational titles. The National Council for the Social Studies (NCSS; www.socialstudies.org) aims to prepare students for college, career, and citizenship. Through conferences, publications, and online resources, the NCSS gives elementary teachers and subject-specific social studies and history teachers the tools to support their professional development. The association's website offers the National Curriculum Standards for Social Studies: The Themes of Social Studies.[1] The themes and strands include the following:

- Culture
- Time, continuity, and change
- People, places, and environments
- Individual development and identity
- Individual groups and institutions
- Power, authority, and governance
- Production, distribution, and consumption
- Science, technology, and society
- Global connections
- Civic ideals and practices

The general nature of these broad topics can be integrated into lesson plans throughout the K–12 continuum and demonstrate how instructional goals connect with overarching themes.

In collaboration with the Children's Book Council (www.cbcbooks.org), the NCSS produces the annual "Notable Social Studies Trade Books for Young People," an annotated list that features titles representing excellence. For 2009, one of the selected titles was *The Boy Who Dared: A Novel Based on the True Story of a Hitler Youth*, by Susan Campbell Bartoletti. This World War II story is a fine audiobook, produced by Listening Library and narrated by David Ackroyd, that connects with several of the NCSS's themes. Selections of other works appearing on the annual list can be found in chapters 4–7.

NATIONAL SCIENCE TEACHERS ASSOCIATION

The mission of the National Science Teachers Association (NSTA; www.nsta.org) is to promote excellence and innovation in science teaching and learning for all. The support that the NSTA gives to science professionals, from elementary school through college, is extensive, from lesson plans to conferences and publications, and the association offers strong advocacy for science education.

One resource that is available on the association's website is the NSTA Learning Center, where teachers can select a science topic, a grade level, and their state, whereupon a listing is presented that gives that state's science standards for that grade level.

For more than thirty-five years, the NSTA and the Children's Book Council have collaborated to select the annual Outstanding Science Trade Books for Students, K–12. The titles are grouped by science topics, such as physical science, life science, science in personal and social perspectives, science and technology, and history and nature of science. An example from the 2010 list is *Almost Astronauts: 13 Women Who Dared to Dream*, by Tanya Lee Stone; this is a fine audiobook, performed by Susan Ericksen and produced by Brilliance Audio.

As we will see in the following four chapters of annotated lists of audiobooks, it is easy to integrate science topics with learning standards for many suggested science lessons.

NATIONAL COUNCIL OF TEACHERS OF MATHEMATICS

The mission of the National Council of Teachers of Mathematics (NCTM; www.nctm.org), as stated on the council's website, is "to be a public voice of mathematics education supporting teachers to ensure equitable mathematics learning of the highest quality for all students through vision, leadership, professional development and research." The breadth of resources for mathematics educators is extensive and includes (as with the previous subject associations) conferences, publications, lessons, and professional development opportunities. The NCTM is actively supporting teachers as they plan to implement the Common Core Mathematics Standards, an indication that the effort to consolidate standards in this subject is moving forward. Mathematics concepts are present in audiobook titles that we feature, which can be used to support instructional activities and themes.

Additional National Subject Associations

There are numerous other subject area associations, such as the National Art Education Association (http://arteducators.org), the National Association for Music Education (www.menc.org), the National Association for Gifted Children (www.nagc.org), the National Association of Special Education Teachers (www.naset.org), the American Association for Health Education (www.aahperd.org/aahe/), the National Association for Sport and Physical Education (www.aahperd.org/naspe/), and the American Council on the Teaching of Foreign Language (www.actfl .org), which provide guidance and professional development resources for teaching staff. These associations' inclusion of some subject topics that are not featured in the Common Core is helpful for educators and librarians. This is by no means an exhaustive list but an indication of how many specific curriculum topics are represented in our work to integrate audiobooks into subject-based standards.

National Associations and Educational Reform Initiatives

THE PARTNERSHIP FOR 21ST CENTURY SKILLS

The Partnership for 21st Century Skills (www.p21.org) represents more than forty member organizations, ranging from Apple to the American Association of School Librarians, Lego Microsoft, *Sesame Street*, and Verizon. The partnership has created the Framework for 21st Century Learning, which addresses the following topics: core subjects and twenty-first century themes, learning and innovation skills, information, media and technology skills, and life and career skills.[2]

This is an important initiative to highlight the effort of bringing learning standards to the national level and how using audiobooks addresses many instructional themes.

AMERICAN ASSOCIATION OF SCHOOL LIBRARIANS

The American Association of School Librarians (www.ala.org/aasl), a division of the American Library Association, has developed and published *Standards for the 21st Century Learner*. Although the core of these standards centers on information literacy, the stated skills can also be correlated with listening to audiobooks. A brief example:

1—Inquire, think critically and gain knowledge:

Skills:

1.1.6   Read, view and listen for information presented in any format (e.g., textual, visual, media, digital) in order to make inferences and gather meaning.

These standards serve as an additional layer of student learning standards at the national level.

Formerly the Association for Supervision and Curriculum Development, ASCD (www.ascd.org) has as its mission statement: "ASCD is a membership organization that develops programs, products, and services essential to the way educators learn, teach, and lead."[3] This professional organization provides developments in the field of education, reform initiatives, and practical resources for teachers and administrators at all levels. Especially active in the advocacy of education reform, ASCD is well known for several education programs, such as Understanding by Design by Grant Wiggins and Jay McTighe, a guide for designing curriculum and instruction that has developed a wide following, with online courses, additional support publications, and conference and workshop presentations.[4] Books, journals, conferences, online courses, education research, and policy positions put ASCD in a prominent position in the field of education. Its work supports effective teaching and learning nationwide by overseeing curriculum development, and we integrate its information into the use of audiobooks as an effective medium for instruction.

PRINCIPLES FOR LEARNING: A FOUNDATION FOR TRANSFORMING K–12 EDUCATION

A collaboration among several prestigious associations has resulted in the twelve-point "Principles for Learning."[5] The organizations include the National Council for the Social Studies, the National Council for Teachers of Mathematics, the National Science Teachers Association, the National Council of Teachers of English, the Consortium for School Networking, and the Association for Career and Technical Education. The principles are general in nature but give solid guidance for use with students. They provide interest to the topic of instructional standards because of the wide collaboration they represent and the clear goals for curriculum planning. They can be used to support many lessons and units for classrooms and libraries; for example, the first principle is "being literate is at the heart of learning in every subject area."[6] We believe that audiobooks certainly demonstrate the goal of becoming literate in every subject area.

NATIONAL CENTER ON UNIVERSAL DESIGN FOR LEARNING

The National Center on Universal Design for Learning (UDL; www .udlcenter.org) provides curricula, guidelines, and support for educators to build on serving the learning needs of all students. The UDL is a scientifically valid framework for guiding educational practice that

(A) provides flexibility in the ways information is presented, in the ways students respond or demonstrate knowledge and skills, and in the ways students are engaged; and

(B) reduces barriers in instruction, provides appropriate accommodations, supports, and challenges, and maintains high achievement expectations for all students, including students with disabilities and students who are limited English proficient.[7]

State Curriculum Standards

Here is a small listing (in alphabetical order) with examples of individual state learning standards, including states that have adopted the Common Core. Since the Common Core was developed and drafted in 2009–2010, many states face decisions to align with these national standards or to remain with their own. This is especially relevant for social studies, as most states have designed specific state history curriculum and grade-level standards. This brief discussion serves to highlight the breadth of resources that can assist educators in their curriculum planning. The focus here is to investigate how the standards align with the integration of audiobooks into instruction.

CALIFORNIA

The California Department of Education (www.cde.ca.gov) has adopted the Common Core, but it also references its own content standards, thus giving educators, librarians, and parents an opportunity to compare the individual state learning standards with the Common Core. Many states face this transition, and this is an important time for student learning expectations. Here is a brief comparison of a California Standard for grade 1 and a Common Core Standard for grade 1, both of which could integrate audiobooks into instruction:

California—Grade 1—English Language Arts

1.0   Listening and Speaking Strategies
      Students listen critically and respond appropriately to oral
      communication.

Common Core State Standards—English Language Arts—K–5
      Speaking and Listening—Grade 1

      Ask and answer questions about key details in a text read aloud or
      information presented orally or through other media.

Educators, when designing specific language arts lessons, could choose
either of these standards to use audiobooks with students.

COLORADO

The Colorado Department of Education (www.cde.state.co.us) has
adopted the Common Core. However, it has also developed documents
that provide a transition from the Colorado Academic Standards to the
Common Core and that demonstrate the similarities and differences
between the two. The Colorado Department of Education states, "These
documents represent the integration of the combined academic content
of both sets of standards, maintaining the unique aspects of the CAS
(Colorado Academic Standards), which include personal financial literacy, 21st century skills, school readiness competencies, postsecondary
and workforce readiness competencies, and preschool expectations."[8]

FLORIDA

The Florida Department of Education (www.fldoe.org) has adopted the
Common Core, but as do other states, it also continues to use its state
standards during a transition time. Florida's detailed standards for English language arts include strands for reading process, literary analysis,
writing process, writing applications, communication and information,
and media literacy. The Common Core English Language Arts Standards for K–5 include literature, informational text, foundational skills,
writing, and speaking and listening. Comparisons between the Common Core and Florida's standards present some challenges in topics and
grade levels.[9]

MASSACHUSETTS

The Massachusetts Department of Elementary and Secondary Education (www.doe.mass.edu) has developed, in response to the Common

Core, "The Massachusetts Framework for English Language Arts and Literacy: Incorporating the Common Core State Standards for English Language Arts and Literacy in History/Social Studies, Science, and Technical Subjects."[10] This 130-page document incorporates and correlates both sets of standards. As an example, for reading standards for literature for grade 6, both the Common Core and the "Massachusetts Framework" adopt the integration-of-knowledge standard:

> 7. Compare and contrast the experience of reading a story, drama, or poem to listening to or viewing an audio, video, or live version of the text, including contrasting what they "see" and "hear" when reading the text to what they perceive when they listen or watch.

However, in some instances, Massachusetts added a specific detail, such as knowledge of language in grade 6:

> 3. Use knowledge of language when writing, speaking, reading or listening
>   a. Vary sentence patterns for meaning, reader/listener interest and style[11]

The "Massachusetts Framework" also builds on the Common Core for recommended literature titles, adding the significant lists "Suggested Contemporary Authors and Illustrators" and "Suggested Authors in World Literature." This comprehensive framework serves to highlight states' efforts to align their learning standards with the Common Core.

NEW YORK

The New York State Education Department (www.nysed.gov) has adopted the Common Core but, like many other states, has incorporated and adapted some of its individual standards.[12] As New York clearly describes: "This document includes all of the Common Core State Standards in English Language Arts and Literacy plus the New York recommended additions approved on January 10, 2011. All of the New York State additions to the Common Core are highlighted under the related strand (reading, writing, speaking and listening, and language) or standard."[13]

For the K–5 Anchor Standards for Writing, New York has added an important standard to the Common Core:

> Responding to Literature
> 11. Develop personal, cultural, textual, and thematic connections within and across genres as they respond to texts through written, digital, and oral presentations, employing a variety of media and genres.

Therefore, locating which specific standard will best serve student learning, especially when considering literacy skills, is important to the goal of audiobooks for instructional use.

OHIO

The Ohio Department of Education (www.ode.state.oh.us) has also developed transitional material to compare the K–12 Ohio Academic Content Standards with the Common Core Standards. To highlight how complicated this task is, here is a comparison of the grade 4 language arts standards for speaking and listening:

> Common Core State Standard—Paraphrase portions of a text read aloud or information presented in diverse media and formats, including visually, quantitatively, and orally.

> Ohio Academic Content Standard—Grade 5—Organize information in a systemic way

However, the Ohio Department of Education states this proviso:

> Because benchmarks and grade-level indicators . . . are not equivalent to the Common Core State Standards, the alignment between the two is not perfect and should not be used to re-purpose curriculum and instructional materials. Curricular planning should not be done with the crosswalk document alone; educators also should plan to use the model curricula which will be available in the spring of 2011. The model curricula will include content elaborations that further clarify the parameters of the standard statements.[14]

Integrating instructional lessons with learning standards presents both opportunities and challenges for teaching staff in comparing national, state, and local guidelines for curriculum planning.

TEXAS

As of this writing (early 2011), the Texas Education Agency (www .tea.state.tx.us) has not adopted the Common Core, and instead uses the Texas Essential Knowledge and Skills (TEKS) for curriculum guidelines. For social studies, each grade level of TEKS presents a comprehensive structure of learning goals with topics that reflect the themes of history, geography, economics, government, citizenship, culture, science technology and society, and social studies skills.[15] However, here is one example, for grade 4, that exemplifies the dilemma that individual states have with the Common Core, as the history guideline for this grade specifically focuses on Texas history:

> (3) History. The student understands the importance of the Texas Revolution, the Republic of Texas, and the annexation of Texas to the United States. The student is expected to:
>
> (A) analyze the causes, major events, and effects of the Texas Revolution, including the Battle of the Alamo, the Texas Declaration of Independence, the Runaway Scrape, and the Battle of San Jacinto.[16]

For English language arts and reading, the grade 2 learning standards are very detailed and explicit, building a continuum from kindergarten through grade 5 at the elementary level. In grade 2, the following standard demonstrates how audiobooks support literacy skills:

> (9) Reading/Comprehension of Literary Text/Fiction. Students understand, make inferences and draw conclusions about the structure and elements of fiction and provide evidence from text to support their understanding. Students are expected to:
>
> (A) describe similarities and differences in the plots and settings of several works by the same author; and (B) describe main characters in works of fiction, including their traits, motivations, and feelings.[17]

As the review of individual states continues, the variations between grade levels and subjects provide an interesting overview for educators.

VIRGINIA

The Virginia Department of Education (www.doe.virginia.gov) is one of the states that continues to update its Standards of Learning while providing guidance about the Common Core.[18] As an example, Virginia revised its English Language Arts Standards of Learning in October 2010 to provide a crosswalk between the two documents. Seeing the two sets of standards, national and state, side by side, gives both comparison and guidance to educators. As an illustration of this, the Common Core's key ideas and details for grade 8 in reading for literature states:

> 3. Analyze how particular lines of dialogue or incidents in a story or drama propel the action, reveal aspects of a character, or provoke a decision.

In contrast, the Virginia Standard of Learning correlates and adds several detailed strands that integrate well with the features of listening to an audiobook:

> 8.5 The student will read and analyze a variety of fictional texts, narrative nonfiction, and poetry.
>
> 8.5 d) Understand the author's use of conventional elements and characteristics within a variety of genres.
>
> 8.5 e) Compare and contrast the author's use of word choice, dialogue, form, rhyme, rhythm, and voice in different texts.
>
> 8.5 f) Analyze how particular lines of dialogue or incidents in a story or drama propel the action, reveal aspects of a character, or provoke a decision.

So, it appears that the adoption of the Common Core has provided an opportunity for many states to revise, compare, and integrate individual state standards with the national effort to standardize student learning expectations in grades K–12.

Local Examples of Curriculum Standards

With the implementation and adoption of the Common Core State Standards, and many states transitioning their content standards, it is interesting to note that local school districts are developing curriculum guidelines and learning objectives for their teaching staff. The following sections provide some examples of local guidelines for instructional practice for both large and small jurisdictions.

ATLANTA PUBLIC SCHOOLS, GEORGIA

With more than ninety schools and programs, the Atlanta Public Schools (www.atlanta.k12.ga.us) serve approximately fifty thousand students. The Common Core State Standards were adopted in 2010, and the Georgia Department of Education is transitioning standards to the Georgia Common Core Performance Standards. For the Atlanta Public Schools, this provides a number of access points to determine learning expectations at each grade level. As an example, the Atlanta Social Studies Department has a grade K–12 curriculum overview that gives a brief description of what is studied at each grade. This is very useful for librarians and parents, but teaching staff use the Georgia Department of

Education guidelines, including the Common Core. This local example serves to demonstrate the current fluidity of learning standards at the national, state, and local levels.

BELCHERTOWN PUBLIC SCHOOLS, MASSACHUSETTS

The Belchertown Public Schools (www.belchertownps.org) represents a small western Massachusetts district, with one high school, one middle school, and three elementary schools, and a total of 2,700 students. Massachusetts has adopted the Common Core State Standards, and Belchertown has aligned its curriculum program guides to support the Common Core and the "Massachusetts Framework." For grade 3 language arts, at the Swift River Elementary School, an illustration of one academic goal is "Listening Skills and Strategies: Listen for a purpose; Listen for enjoyment; Listen to a variety of media and speakers." The development of a detailed curriculum that correlates and addresses national, state, and local academic goals is clearly demonstrated and acknowledges the breadth of learning standards.

CHICAGO PUBLIC SCHOOLS, ILLINOIS

The Chicago Public Schools (www.cps.edu) is the third-largest school district in the nation, with 675 schools and more than four hundred thousand students. The Chicago Public Schools example highlights the effort to locate the correct path for district standards: the actual link to curriculum guidelines for the Chicago Public Schools is at the Office of Teaching and Learning (www.chicagoteachingandlearning.org), and there appears to be no visible link from the main Chicago site. However, perseverance prevails for researchers—all core curricular subjects are represented here: language arts, social studies, math, and science. Illinois has also adopted the Common Core, and educators in Chicago may choose the Illinois Learning Standards, the Common Core, or guidance from the Chicago Social Science Department. The focus of each subject and grade level is listed. As an example, in kindergarten, the theme is "Myself and Others." For educators, librarians, and parents, finding the current status of learning standards for a specific grade level or subject is part of integrating instructional design with student expectations.

MADISON METROPOLITAN SCHOOL DISTRICT, WISCONSIN

The Madison Metropolitan School District (www.madison.k12.wi.us) includes forty-eight schools with a student population of approximately

twenty-four thousand. In keeping with the target of audiobooks supporting literacy, language arts and literacy serve as the curriculum subject to
illustrate local standards. Wisconsin has also adopted the Common Core,
and the Madison schools have published language arts performance
standards. However, as of early 2011, the website did not include references to the Common Core but provided the school district's standards,
which combine both the current Wisconsin standards and the Madison
additions. One of the most interesting statements includes the following,
which directly applies to the use of audiobooks in instructional settings:

> Finally, although there are six State of Wisconsin Language Arts Stan-
> dards, we chose to combine and integrate the language and technology
> standards. This reflects our belief that literacy skills connect across all
> academic areas. "To use media, one must read or listen. To write, one must
> acquire knowledge by reading, listening, and viewing. To do research, one
> must read. To communicate in any form, one must know how the language
> works." Since all communication has content, the [Madison Metropoli-
> tan School District] Language Arts Standards are closely connected to all
> other content areas and technology is an integral part of all that we do in
> 21st century learning.[19]

For the purpose of linking learning standards with audiobooks, the statement recognizes that listening is a critical skill for literacy.

MONTGOMERY COUNTY PUBLIC SCHOOLS, MARYLAND

The Montgomery County Public Schools (www.montgomeryschoolsmd
.org) is the largest school system in Maryland and the sixteenth largest
in the nation, with two hundred schools and more than 140,000 students.
Maryland has adopted the Common Core, but the Montgomery school
system has updated and clearly stated its position regarding local, state,
and national standards with this statement from its English language
arts program: "Guided by the Maryland English Language Arts Content
Standards (2008) and the Common Core State Standards for English
Language Arts (2010), the Pre-K-12 English Language Arts program
focuses on the communication processes of reading, writing, speaking,
listening, and viewing through the study of language and literature."[20]
The district's online portal provides clear links to the Common Core
and to the district curriculum framework. Here is an elementary content
statement for the English Language Arts Framework that connects with
the use of audiobooks:

Reading and Listening—Effective readers and listeners use strategies before, during, and after reading or listening to construct and extend meaning according to the text and purpose. They access background knowledge, survey structure, predict, question, summarize, clarify, visualize, draw conclusions, validate perceptions, analyze, synthesize, and evaluate. In English Language Arts classes, students develop and apply these strategies to a variety of increasingly challenging and complex texts.[21]

SEATTLE PUBLIC SCHOOLS

The Seattle Public Schools (http://district.seattleschools.org) is the largest K–12 school system in the state of Washington, serving forty-seven thousand students in ninety-one schools. Information about academic standards is located in the "Instructional Services" section of the Seattle Public Schools' website. The local school system has acknowledged and adapted its goals for student learning by creating a document that realigns its Language Arts Essential Reading Standards for grades 9–12 with both the College Board Standards for College Success and the Common Core Standards. (As of early 2011, Washington had not adopted the Common Core.) Here is a brief example of a grade 11 strand for language arts that demonstrates the recognition of the Common Core with local goals:

Integration of Knowledge and Ideas:
> Compare and Contrast across Mediums:

>> Compare and contrast multiple interpretations of a drama or story (e.g., recorded or live productions) distinguishing how each version interprets the source text. (Secondary Standard Modified Common Core). Listening to an audiobook demonstrates this learning goal.

CONCLUSION

The availability of national, state, and local curriculum standards for student learning is facilitated by online technology that enables teachers, librarians, and parents to access this information easily. Reliance on a framework that builds from kindergarten through high school creates a continuum for students across the nation to have some consistency in their education. Using audiobooks to achieve instructional goals is based on research and good instructional objectives. The efforts of educators to develop such learning standards highlight the goals of educating our nation's children.

~~~~~~

Whether my students are reluctant readers or voracious ones, offering a wide selection of audiobook choices allows my teens the opportunity to choose which way they want to experience a great story. Allowing teens to "plug in" as a way to engage with great books will motivate them to enjoy novels and literature they may have been unwilling to try out before. For many of the students I serve, audiobooks are seen as an appealing, alternative format to printed books. Supporting listening as a valid educational experience can help move students down a path where literacy and achievement will come together to bridge gaps that may currently exist in their reading abilities. One thing for me is clear—offering (and widely promoting) a diverse audiobook collection offers students a way to connect with books in a way that is both highly engaging and richly rewarding.

—Rose Brock, school librarian, Coppell Middle School West, Coppell Independent School District, Coppell, Texas

~~~~~~

In the following chapters we have provided many examples of standards that connect the theme of an audiobook with an instructional objective. These examples are paraphrased or reworded from national, state, and local standards that we have discussed in this chapter and researched and investigated for many years. Our examples represent how educators use these goals when designing student lessons.

NOTES

1. National Council for the Social Studies, "National Curriculum Standards for Social Studies: The Themes of Social Studies,"http://www.socialstudies.org/standards/strands.

2. Partnership for 21st Century Skills, *Framework for 21st Century Learning*, www.p21.org/index.php?option=com_content&task=view&id=254&Itemid=120.

3. ASCD, "ASCD's 2008–2011 Strategic Plan," http://www.ascd.org/about_ascd/Governance/Strategic_Plan/Strategic_Plan_-_2008.aspx

4. Grant Wiggins and Jay McTighe, Understanding by Design, http://www.ascd.org/research-a-topic/understanding-by-design-resources.aspx.

5. National Council of Teachers of Mathematics, "Principles for Learning," www.nctm.org/.../Research.../Principles_for_Learning_May_2010.pdf.

6. Ibid.

7. UDL, www.udlcenter.org.

8. Colorado Department of Education, "Colorado P-12 Academic Standards," http://www.cde.state.co.us/cdeassess/UAS/CoAcademicStandards.html.

9. For the Common Core, see www.corestandards.org; for Florida, see Florida Department of Education, "Next Generation Sunshine State Standards," http://www.fldoe.org/bii/Curriculum/SSS/.

10. Massachusetts Department of Education, "Massachusetts Framework for English Language Arts and Literacy: Incorporating the Common Core State Standards for English Language Arts and Literacy in History/Social Studies, Science, and Technical Subjects," http://www.doe.mass.edu/candi/commoncore.

11. Ibid.

12. See New York State Education Department, "NYS P-12 Common Core Learning Standards," www.p12.nysed.gov/ciai/common_core_standards.

13. Ibid.

14. Ohio Department of Education, "Comparison of the K–12 Ohio Academic Content Standards and the Common Core Standards," http://www.ode.state .oh.us/GD/Templates/Pages/ODE/ODEDetail.aspx?page=3&TopicRelationID =1699&ContentID=92009.

15. Texas Education Agency, "Chapter 113: Texas Essential Knowledge and Skills for Social Studies; Subchapter A: Elementary," http://ritter.tea.state .tx.us/rules/tac/chapter113/ch113a.html.

16. Ibid.

17. Texas Education Agency, "Chapter 110: Texas Essential Knowledge and Skills for English Language Arts and Reading; Subchapter A. Elementary," http://ritter.tea.state.tx.us/rules/tac/chapter110/ch110a.html.

18. Virginia Department of Education, "Virginia Standards of Learning and Common Core State Standards," www.doe.virginia.gov/testing/common_ core/index.shtml.

19. Madison Metropolitan School District, "Grade Level Standards, K–5, Introduction," http://readingweb.madison.k12.wi.us.

20. Montgomery County Public Schools, "English Language Arts Framework," http://www.montgomeryschoolsmd.org/uploadedFiles/curriculum/english/ homepage/English%20Language%20Arts%20Framework.pdf.

21. Montgomery County Public Schools, "English Language Arts Framework," http://www.montgomeryschoolsmd.org/curriculum/english.

4

Audiobooks and Primary School

Grades K–2

*T*he titles in this chapter support literacy in a variety of ways. For example, picture books (a staple of early elementary classrooms) in a read-along format offer an excellent means of acquiring both visual and print literacy skills. The purpose of a read-along is to allow children to follow the story through text and illustrations without the burden of decoding. Read-alongs model fluency, provide an opportunity for increasing vocabulary, and give children the time to "read" the illustrations, thereby supporting the Common Core, which encourages primary students to use the illustrations to describe the details in the text and to explain how the illustrations might clarify and enhance the text.

In addition, because audiobooks remove the need to decode unfamiliar or difficult words, read-alongs foster increased development of what the Common Core refers to as an "understanding and working knowledge of concepts of print."[1] Read-alongs permit children to discern that words are read from left to right, that the words on the page represent the spoken language they are hearing, and that sentences are read with inflection and are set apart by capitalization and punctuation.

The chapter books selected here for the primary grades also encourage greater development of comprehension, vocabulary, and fluency. Studies show that children can listen and comprehend literature two to three levels above their actual ability to read, which makes read-aloud titles (as opposed to read-along titles) also an integral part of the early elementary classroom. What could be more effective than listening to a chapter book read with expert pacing, clarity, pronunciation, and emotion? Busy teachers will enjoy having these titles at their disposal.

In this and the other chapters pairing audiobook titles and learning standards, you will find sprinkled throughout several instances of Common Core text exemplars. These texts are designed to "exemplify the level of complexity and quality that the Standards require all students in a given grade band to engage with. Additionally, they are suggestive of the breadth of text that students should encounter in the text types required by the Standards. The choices should serve as useful guideposts in helping educators select texts of similar complexity, quality, and range for their own classrooms."[2]

Parents will also find these titles useful in home settings. The story and art in these read-alongs can engage children, and by listening to the tracks with the page-turn signals, they will easily be able to follow along with little or no adult intervention. We often tell kindergarteners and first graders to check these titles out for when they're in the mood for a story and their grown-up is too busy to read to them. Read-alongs also work particularly well in families where the adults may not be fluent English-language readers themselves.

Chapter books, too, are valuable for home listening. Try them when everyone is in the kitchen preparing dinner or running errands in the car. They will provide a satisfying shared listening experience and will help cut down on time spent in front of the television or computer. We also know of many families who encourage their children to listen to audiobooks at bedtime—with the lights off.

The following titles fulfill these and many other instructional tenets for primary grade teachers to share with their students, as well as for families to enjoy together at home. *Note: For those books designed as read-alongs, we include the illustrator in the citation and mark them with an asterisk after the title.*

One little guy told me he loves to listen to audiobooks "because it seems more real." Audiobooks are a pretty spectacular way to experience even more of the story than you could by reading it yourself—you often get to hear the voice of the writer.

—Jon Scieszka, children's book author and 2008 Library of Congress
Ambassador for Young People's Literature

26 Fairmount Avenue, written and narrated by Tomie dePaola,
Listening Library

Tomie de Paola, the well-known author and illustrator, narrates this Newbery Honor autobiographical story. He takes the listener back to his childhood, recounting the small excitements surrounding family life, starting school and building a new home, the construction of which is interrupted by the arrival of a hurricane. The author's calm and comforting voice lends special importance to the story. The child's perspective is always kept in these short biographies and will be enjoyed by dePaola's many young fans, as it encourages them to tell or write their own life experiences. For those students who choose to follow along with the print edition, dePaola's charming black-and-white illustrations will add to the enjoyment. The audiobook package includes the first four books in dePaola's extensive autobiographical series: *26 Fairmount Avenue, Here We All Are, On My Way,* and *What a Year.*

STANDARD—ENGLISH LANGUAGE ARTS
Students retell an event or sequence of events from a book they have read, detailing action, emotions, event order, and closure.

The Arnold Lobel Collection, written by Arnold Lobel, narrated
by Mark Linn-Baker, HarperChildren's Audio

Linn-Baker's exquisite pacing and precise, comfortable narration give perfect voice to Lobel's enchanting stories, allowing listeners to revel in the emotions and ironic humor of these easy reader gems. Owl's foolish fears, Uncle Elephant's caring reassurance to his frightened nephew, the unusual characters whom Grasshopper meets on his journey, and Small Pig's misadventures in the city all relate to children's own experiences. Jaunty music begins and ends the audiobook, further enhancing the aural experience. The collection includes *Owl at Home, Grasshopper on the Road, Uncle Elephant,* and *Small Pig. Owl at Home* is a Common Core text exemplar for grades K–1.

STANDARD—ENGLISH LANGUAGE ARTS
Students will be able to describe the characters in a story and explain their feelings and actions.

Bear Snores On, * written and narrated by Karma Wilson,
   illustrated by Jane Chapman, Weston Woods

Bear has hunkered down for his long winter rest, but his forest friends have other ideas for using his cave. As Bear snores on (and on and on), the other animals stay warm in the den, sharing good food and fun. When Bear is awakened by sneeze-provoking pepper from Mouse's stew, he joins in the fun, only to have his friends fall asleep. Wilson inhabits each of her creatures with just the right timbre and pacing. Music and sound effects round out this whimsical, cozy introduction to classroom discussions of animal habitats.

STANDARD—SCIENCE
Students will understand that animals have basic needs from their environment.

Brown Bear, Brown Bear, What Do You See? * written by Bill
   Martin Jr., illustrated by Eric Carle, narrated by Gwyneth
   Paltrow and others, Macmillan Audio

One of the most loved picture books for teaching predictability, this read-along works exceptionally well in audio. Three separate narrations are available on the disc: one read with charming animal personification by Paltrow accompanied by a chorus of children; one read by the late author with a robust pacing that emphasizes the repetition; and a sprightly, carefully articulated Spanish version. Kindergarteners will enjoy listening to this again and again.

STANDARD—ENGLISH LANGUAGE ARTS
Students will use pictures to make predictions and will participate in activities using stories with repeated patterns.

Buttons for General Washington, * written by Peter Roop and
   Connie Roop, illustrated by Peter E. Hanson, narrated by
   Jason Harris, Live Oak Media

Fourteen-year-old John Darragh was one of our country's earliest spies—working for the revolutionary forces against the British army. Carrying his message to General Washington concealed in his coat buttons, Darragh faces a terrible fate—possible hanging—when he loses a button and is captured. Background music and sound effects, including a fife-

and-drum corps and the clomping of horse's hooves, combine with Harris's expert pacing to heighten the tension and excitement of the narrative. An authors' note explains the spy efforts of Darragh and his Quaker family, which increases the instructional value of this slice of American history.

STANDARDS—ENGLISH LANGUAGE ARTS AND HISTORY/SOCIAL STUDIES
Students will describe historical events in an informational text; students will be able to identify the role of historical figures, such as George Washington.

Caps for Sale: A Tale of a Peddler, Some Monkeys, and Their Monkey Business,* written and illustrated by Esphyr Slobodkina, narrated by Peter Fernandez, Live Oak Media

Children will relish the adventures of a hungry peddler who carries his caps on his head—sorted by color. After taking a nap under a tree, the peddler wakes to discover that monkeys have stolen every cap. How is he to get them back? Background music and an expertly paced reading will draw children into this comical picture-book classic while they learn to count and sort by color.

STANDARD—MATHEMATICS
Students will learn counting, cardinality, classification; students will answer "how many" questions in regards to sets of objects.

Celia Cruz: Queen of Salsa,* written by Veronica Chambers, illustrated by Julie Maren, narrated by Michelle Manzo, Live Oak Media

An authentic musical background captures young listeners and draws them into the life of the Cuban salsa singer. The tropical flavor, the story of Celia's rise to fame, and the inclusion of her singing one of her songs make this a good choice for celebrating Latino heritage. Sound effects and vocal flourishes support the flow of the story, with Manzo's excellent performance adding to the cultural authenticity. Spanish pronunciations are on target and give a palpable "you are there" atmosphere. Cruz's contributions to music are a good platform for encouraging young people to explore their own talents.

STANDARD—THE ARTS
Students understand how personal and cultural forces influence the arts.

Charlie Needs a Cloak,* written and illustrated by Tomie dePaola,
    narrated by Gene Deitch, Weston Woods

Charlie the shepherd really needs a new cloak—his old one is torn and tattered. So he goes about making himself a new one: he shears the sheep, he cleans and cards the wool, he spins it into yarn, he dyes the yarn and weaves it into fabric, then he cuts and sews the fabric into a lovely new cloak. All the while one of Charlie's sheep keeps interfering in ways that are sure to make children giggle as they "read" the pictures. Music, sound effects, and spirited narration contribute to make this a classroom hit.

STANDARD—ENGLISH LANGUAGE ARTS
Students will be able to describe characters and events in a story.

Charlie Parker Played Be Bop,* written and illustrated
    by Chris Raschka, narrated by Richard Allen,
    Live Oak Media

This read-along package immerses children in the music of jazz legend Charlie Parker. An introduction by the author-illustrator explains how he represented Parker's music through words and pictures. Allen both reads and sings the text, accompanied by jazz riffs from an old recording of Parker's "A Night in Tunisia," which the book celebrates, in a production that elevates and expands on Raschka's innovative book, allowing young listeners to fully understand what be bop is all about.

STANDARD—MUSIC
Students characterize music and musicians from a variety of historical and cultural settings.

Chicken Little,* by Rebecca and Ed Emberley, narrated by Walter
    Mayes, Weston Woods

This madcap retelling of Chicken Licken begs to be read aloud, and Mayes is more than up to the task. When a falling acorn knocks the hapless Chicken Little senseless (although there wasn't much sense in him to begin with), he immediately assumes the worst—"Oh my goodness, oh my gracious! The sky is falling! The sky is falling!" Mayes employs a distinctly ridiculous voice for each of the outlandishly witless fowl that end up running for their lives, right into the "warm, dark cave" of Foxy Loxy's welcoming mouth. The droll text and comical illustrations lend themselves to this over-the-top production that highlights the advisability of always having a plan. A concluding interview with Ed Emberley provides insight into the creative process of making picture books.

STANDARD—ENGLISH LANGUAGE ARTS
Students will ask questions before, during, and after reading or listening to a story.

A Child's Calendar,* written and narrated by John Updike,
   illustrated by Trina Schart Hyman, Live Oak Media

Twelve child-centered poems—one for each month of the year—represent the changing seasons through observations of the natural world as well as celebrations throughout the year. Hyman's saturated watercolor paintings depict a multiracial cast living somewhere in rural New England and serve as the perfect complement to Updike's elegantly understated narration. The quiet, even pacing will allow children to easily follow the poetic format.

STANDARDS—ENGLISH LANGUAGE ARTS AND SCIENCE
Students will be able to identify words that rhyme; students will investigate and understand patterns in their daily lives.

Chrysanthemum,* written and illustrated by Kevin Henkes,
   narrated by Meryl Streep, Weston Woods

What could be worse than discovering that the name you've always thought to be perfect has become the center of merciless teasing? Such is the plight of new kindergartener, Chrysanthemum, one of Henkes's early mouse children. Streep's perfect sense of timing and vocal dexterity create wholly believable characters, especially the annoying "mean girls" Victoria, Rita, and Jo. With the help of her beloved music teacher, Mrs. Delphinium Twinkle, Chrysanthemum regains her confidence and triumphs over the bullies. Spirited musical accompaniment heightens the listening pleasure.

STANDARD—HISTORY/SOCIAL STUDIES
Students will practice honesty, self-control, and kindness to others.

Clementine, written by Sara Pennypacker, narrated by Jessica
    Almasy, Recorded Books

Third grade is fraught with danger for the intrepid Clementine. She tries so hard at everything, but nothing seems to go right—not school, not friendships, and certainly not family life. "Okay, fine" is her response to all of these troubles. Almasy makes this refrain, as well as the rest of Clementine's narrative, sparkle with flawless eight-year-old pitch and pacing. Fortunately for listeners, Clementine's further adventures are also available on audio.

STANDARD—HISTORY/SOCIAL STUDIES
Students will recognize the need for rules and will learn to accept responsibility for their actions.

The Collected Stories of Winnie-the-Pooh, written by A. A.
    Milne, narrated by a full cast, Listening Library

Twenty stories from the Pooh pantheon are given full dramatic treatment, with Judi Dench and Michael Williams as superb narrators, giving voice as well to Kanga and Owl, respectively. Stephen Fry is the silly old bear himself, in all his hummy glory; Jane Horrocks captures Piglet's unwavering loyalty; and Geoffrey Palmer is in his element as the melancholy Eeyore. Piano melodies accompany Pooh's hums and separate the stories, rounding out an outstanding production of this children's literature classic.

STANDARD—ENGLISH LANGUAGE ARTS
Students will identify problems and solutions when reading or listening to stories.

Dooby, Dooby, Moo,* written by Doreen Cronin, illustrated by
    Betsy Lewin, narrated by Randy Travis, Weston Woods

When Duck finds out about a talent show at the county fair, he and the animals on the farm start rehearsing. While Farmer Brown tries to figure out what the animals are up to, Duck is determined that they will enter the contest and win! Understated, yet hilarious narration and a rollicking musical underbed extend and enhance the story. The inclusion of old rock-and-roll songs like "I Heard It through the Grapevine" and "Born to Be Wild" will ensure that the grown-ups are laughing right along with the kids. A 2008 Odyssey Honor Audiobook.

The Doorbell Rang,* written and illustrated by Pat Hutchins,
    narrated by Suzanne Toren, Live Oak Media

Ma makes a plate of cookies, six each for Victoria and Sam, but when the doorbell rings (cleverly disguised as page-turn signals), the children are forced to practice their counting, proportion, and division skills to share the cookies equally with more and more friends. In this engaging and entertaining look at math skills, narrative and illustrations combine to provide visual clues to Sam and Victoria's feelings as they divide the cookies. Toren's measured narration relieves young listeners from struggling with the reading by reinforcing the repetition of the text and allowing plenty of time to concentrate on the division of the cookies—the central focus of the story.

STANDARD—MATHEMATICS
Students understand the difference between numbers and quantities; they can determine that objects in one group are greater than or smaller than objects in another group.

A Fine, Fine School,* written by Sharon Creech, illustrated and
    narrated by Harry Bliss, Live Oak Media

Lucky Tillie—she goes to a fine, fine school. In fact, she loves going to school, and she loves to learn. Her principal, Mr. Keene, also loves school. In fact, he loves school so much and he loves learning so much that he decides it would be even better if they all went to school *all* the time. Think of all the learning that would happen if school were open on weekends and holidays and during summer vacation! Unfortunately, Mr. Keene's plan has the opposite effect, and Tillie must be brave enough to remind Mr. Keene that learning happens everywhere, not just in school. Bliss's well-paced reading provides plenty of time for listeners to enjoy his humorous illustrations, which detail Creech's text. His use of a megaphone works well with the growing student discontent heard in the background, and other school sound effects add to the fun.

STANDARD—HISTORY/SOCIAL STUDIES
Students will demonstrate confidence in expressing their own beliefs and opinions.

Five Creatures,* written by Emily Jenkins, illustrated by Tomek Bogacki, narrated by Kristen Hahn, Weston Woods

Three humans and two cats make up this young girl's world as she groups her "family" into sets determined by likes, dislikes, and their variety of skills. A sprightly musical bed, appropriately understated sound effects, and a charmingly childlike narration that guides the listener through Bogacki's Venn diagram–like illustrations make this the perfect accompaniment to lessons on counting sets of objects.

STANDARD—MATHEMATICS
Students are able to classify objects by number and category.

The Gardener,* written by Sarah Stewart, illustrated by David Small, narrated by Bonnie Kelley-Young, Live Oak Media

This is the story of Lydia Grace, a young girl who travels away from her country home to live with her dour uncle in the city. Homesick, Lydia writes letters to her family and is pleased to discover window boxes where she can plant some seeds. Her Christmas present of a seed catalog sets the stage for *The Gardener*. Set during the 1930s Depression, the 1998 Caldecott Honor illustrations are a fine companion to this read-along. Lydia Grace's youthful lilt and optimism are clearly present in Kelley-Young's vocal characterization. The narrative brings the listener into a very different time in America's past. (A good pairing for classroom listening is *Miss Bridie Chose a Shovel*; for activity suggestions, see chapter 8.)

STANDARDS—HISTORY/SOCIAL STUDIES AND SCIENCE
Students will learn about urban and rural communities and be able to discuss their common and dissimilar characteristics; students will be able to describe the growing cycle from seed to plant.

The Gooney Bird Collection, written by Lois Lowry, narrated by Lee Adams, Listening Library

From the moment the self-named Gooney Bird Greene enters Mrs. Pigeon's second-grade classroom, nothing is ever the same again. Gooney Bird likes to be "right smack in the middle of things," and she takes center stage immediately. Gooney Bird is a consummate storyteller, and each of the four short novels included in this collection (*Gooney Bird Greene, Gooney Bird and the Room Mother, Gooney the Fabulous,* and *Gooney Bird Is So Absurd*) provides expert instruction on the art of writing for the careful listener. Adams maintains the appropriate pacing and inflection to bring Gooney Bird, her classmates, and the entire school into sharp focus. Her slight Southern accent perfectly defines the main character, and her timing expands the droll cleverness of Lowry's text.

STANDARD—ENGLISH LANGUAGE ARTS

Students will write narratives, recounting events and detailing actions, thoughts, and feelings.

Green Eggs and Ham,* written and illustrated by Dr. Seuss,
 narrated by Jason Alexander, Random House

Repetition and controlled vocabulary are taken to hilarious heights in this classic Seuss early reader. Poor Sam tries valiantly to get his friend to taste his wonderful concoction of green eggs and ham, but he is consistently rebuffed, despite his best rhyming efforts ("Would you eat them in a box? Would you eat them with a fox?"). Dr. Seuss was one of the first author-illustrators to promote the development of phonemic awareness in young children, and his cartoon illustrations always hit the mark by providing visual clues to the meaning of the text. Alexander combines just the right touch of gravitas and humor in his narration, pausing appropriately to allow listeners to absorb the rhythm of the text and the meaning in the pictures. *Green Eggs and Ham* is a Common Core text exemplar for grades K–1.

STANDARD—ENGLISH LANGUAGE ARTS

Students will demonstrate phonemic awareness by using letter and sound relationships to decode unfamiliar words.

Henry Hikes to Fitchburg,* written and illustrated by D. B.
 Johnson, narrated by James Naughton, Weston Woods

In this picture book based on a passage from Henry David Thoreau's *Walden Pond,* Henry and his friend—both represented as bears—agree to travel to and meet in Fitchburg, Massachusetts. While Henry enjoys a leisurely walk, reveling in the natural world around him, his friend works hard to earn his railway fare and arrives in Fitchburg before Henry. Children will find much to discover in the cubist, color-drenched art. Lively music, whistling, and understated narration provide the perfect foil for the complex story and illustrations. The story provides an excellent start to discussions on the nature of work and our relationship with the natural world.

Henry's Freedom Box: A True Story from the Underground Railroad, written by Ellen Levine, illustrated by Kadir Nelson, narrated by Jerry Dixon, Weston Woods

Henry "Box" Brown's courageous story of survival is set during the time of slavery, when families were cruelly torn apart. Henry's flight to freedom is a true and inspiring example of man's instinctive drive for freedom. This audiobook also serves as an excellent example of the read-along format further enhancing listening to a fine performance. Nelson's beautiful illustrations provide students with an opportunity to use their visual literacy skills as they immerse themselves in the emotionally powerful and artistically complex paintings. Dixon's voice is strong and deep, giving the narrative an appropriate pacing and tone. The background music dovetails nicely into specific illustrations—as banjo music plays, Henry is seen playing the banjo, and a mention of Henry humming includes his humming. The resonance of waves splashing when Henry's box is on the boat is one of the compelling sound effects included in the production. An author's note on track 3 gives additional information about the historical background.

Ivy and Bean, written by Annie Barrows, narrated by Cassandra Morris, Recorded Books

Ivy and Bean, two unlikely friends-in-the-making, discover that combining their talents is great fun. When Ivy, a quiet, book-loving girl moves next door to Bean, the proverbial tomboy resists her mother's encouragement to make friends with Ivy. Her resolve dwindles when Ivy helps with a prank involving Bean's older sister Nancy. This is the first in the beginning chapter-book series, and Morris's narration is just right—young and girlish. The girls' conversations are typical of their age, and each chapter presents a separate event so that young listeners can easily enjoy a chapter or two at a time. Ivy and Bean are an appealing combination, and the lively performance heightens their escapades.

STANDARD—ENGLISH LANGUAGE ARTS

Students will be able to describe characters, settings, and major events in a story, and how the main characters solve problems presented to them.

Knuffle Bunny,* written and illustrated by Mo Willems, narrated by Mo Willems, Cheryl Willems, and Trixie Willems, Weston Woods

What begins as a normal trip to the Laundromat leads to near disaster when Dad and Trixie inadvertently leave Knuffle Bunny behind. Poor Dad can't understand the toddler's babblings, but Mom comes to the rescue, averting catastrophe. Every kindergartner will appreciate the angst of losing a treasured toy as the entire Willems family joins together here, elevating this well-loved picture book from a mere print experience to a media event. Even the family pictures are "narrated," with Trixie herself providing the commentary and emotion as the drama enfolds. Dad Mo seems by turns bewildered and frustrated, and Mom Cheryl supplies the calm understanding that saves the day. Music and sound effects round out this thoroughly engaging production.

STANDARD—ENGLISH LANGUAGE ARTS

Students are engaged readers and listeners and can describe the relationship between the illustrations and the story.

Lon Po Po,* written and illustrated by Ed Young, narrated by B. D. Wong, Weston Woods

The wolf at the door may claim to be Po Po, but the three young girls who are home alone soon realize that this deep-voiced stranger is not their grandmother. Their crafty disposal of the malevolent intruder is skillfully told through subtle inflection and deliberate pacing that intensifies the tension of the text and allows plenty of time to pore over the Caldecott-winning illustrations, which are evocative of Chinese panel paintings, in this Red Riding Hood story from China. This title is a Common Core text exemplar for grades K–1.

STANDARD—ENGLISH LANGUAGE ARTS
Students will explain how characters in stories overcome challenges.

---

*Louise, the Adventures of a Chicken,** written by Kate
　　DiCamillo, illustrated by Harry Bliss, narrated by Barbara
　　Rosenblat, Live Oak Media

The escapades of a wandering chicken attain new heights in this fully voiced, drama-filled audio production. Rosenblat milks every ounce of angst and excitement from the intrepid hen's encounters with pirates, circus lions, and nefarious strangers while lively background music and sound effects perfectly match DiCamillo's spare text and Bliss's comical illustrations. Winner of the 2010 Odyssey Medal.

STANDARD—ENGLISH LANGUAGE ARTS
Students will listen to a variety of literary forms, including stories and poems.

Magic Tree House Collection, Books 1–8, written and narrated
　　by Mary Pope Osborne, Listening Library

This collection of the first eight books in the popular Magic Tree House series begins the adventures of Jack and Annie, brother and sister, who travel through time and discover history, solve mysteries, and learn to rely on each other. From the introductory music at the beginning of each book to the author's narration, listeners will become involved with each story, whether it is about dinosaurs, mummies, or pirates. The conversational tone, good pacing, and fairly simple sentences heighten the strengths of the beginning chapter-book format. The voices are differentiated, making it easy for young listeners to distinguish the characters. There is additional interest for students to hear the voice of the author in these stories created to promote the study of history.

STANDARD—ENGLISH LANGUAGE ARTS
Students will compare and contrast stories written by the same author, about similar characters.

---

*Martina, the Beautiful Cockroach: A Cuban Folktale,**
　　retold and narrated by Carmen Agra Deedy, illustrated by
　　Michael Austin, Peachtree Publishers

Unusual but useful advice from her Cuban grandmother helps the lovely Martina determine the worth of her many suitors. Narrated with humor and energy, including a hilarious variety of vocal characterizations, this traditional story is also read in Spanish on another track. A 2009 Odyssey Honor Audiobook.

STANDARD—HISTORY/SOCIAL STUDIES

Materials will be included in classroom instruction that allows students to explore cultural diversity.

Miss Bridie Chose a Shovel,* written by Leslie Connor,
　　illustrated by Mary Azarian, narrated by Katherine Kellgren,
　　Recorded Books

In 1856, Miss Bridie leaves Ireland and sets off for America. Her mother offers her a chiming clock, a porcelain figurine, or a shovel to take on her journey, and the sensible young girl chooses the shovel, setting the course of her practical, hardworking immigrant life. Kellgren's narration is a perfect complement to Connor's unpretentious text and Azarian's sturdy, color-drenched woodblock illustrations. As Miss Bridie uses the shovel to dig into her new life, Kellgren's rich tones and steady pacing allow young listeners ample opportunity to savor each new stage of Bridie's life and enjoy the details of the artwork.

STANDARDS—ENGLISH LANGUAGE ARTS AND HISTORY/SOCIAL STUDIES

Students will describe characters, settings, and major events in a story, using key details; students will understand the concept of chronology and will be able to place events in chronological order.

Mr. Popper's Penguins, written by Richard and Florence Atwater,
　　narrated by Nick Sullivan, Hachette Audio

Mr. Popper loves the polar regions and is surprised to receive a gift of a penguin, which he names Captain Cook. This begins the classic adventures of the house painter who fulfills his dream, and along the way the listener learns about penguins and their habits. From the introductory music that invites the listener into the story to the effective use of sound effects, the humorous, yet informative story remains fresh today. Of special interest is the production of Admiral Drake's radio broadcast, parade music as the penguins march, and the pleasant silliness throughout. This title is a Common Core text exemplar for grades K–1.

STANDARD—SCIENCE

Students understand that living things must live in habitats supporting their needs.

Officer Buckle and Gloria,* written and illustrated by Peggy
  Rathmann, narrated by John Lithgow, Weston Woods

Officer Buckle's safety lessons are so boring that no one pays any
attention, and accidents run rampant at Napville School. So he takes
on a new partner—the exuberant canine Gloria. Attention soars and
accidents disappear. Unfortunately, Officer Buckle discovers that Gloria
is stealing the show, and he stops going to school. When disaster strikes,
he realizes the truth of that most important safety lesson: "Always stick
with your buddy!" Caldecott-winning illustrations, amusing sound
effects, and the counterpoint of forthright narration heighten the humor
and reinforce the message.

STANDARD—PHYSICAL EDUCATION
Students understand and follow safety procedures.

The One and Only Shrek, written by William Steig, narrated by
  Stanley Tucci and Meryl Streep, Macmillan Audio

Because there are no accompanying illustrations to this collection
(*Shrek! Doctor De Soto, Caleb and Kate, Brave Irene, The Amazing
Bone,* and *Spinky Sulks*), all of the listener's attention is focused on
Steig's incredible use of language to paint pictures with words. Tucci's
voicing and pacing perfectly complement Steig's rich language and
complex storytelling, and Streep's enormous vocal range and ability to
create sound effects with her voice lifts even the wind to the level of a
character in this superb production.

STANDARD—ENGLISH LANGUAGE ARTS
Students will listen and respond to stories in a variety of media,
including audiobooks.

Ox-Cart Man,* written and narrated by Donald Hall, illustrated by
  Barbara Cooney, Live Oak Media

Donald Hall, U.S. poet laureate from 2006 to 2007, reads his tale of the
ox-cart man and a year of seasonal life with unadorned, poetic cadence.
Lilting harp and flute music begin the story and continue under Hall's
reading of the title page, fading once the story begins. Cooney's 1980
Caldecott-winning illustrations are in total harmony with Hall's graceful
descriptions of a simpler time, when families lived according to the
dictates of the seasons. The harp alone picks up the opening refrain,

providing a very satisfying conclusion. This story pairs nicely with *A Child's Calendar*, and an activity is suggested in chapter 8.

STANDARD—HISTORY/SOCIAL STUDIES
Students will be able to identify how economics affects individuals, families, and communities.

Rain,* written by Marion Dane Bauer, illustrated by John Wallace, narrated by Paula Parker, (part of the How Our Weather Works series), Live Oak Media

Informational audiobooks give young listeners the ability to listen to subjects they are interested in or are studying in school. In this read-along-format science series, simple facts and short sentences are read clearly with deliberate pacing that provides time for comprehension. The narrator's steady voice keeps the focus on the vocabulary, building the connection from sight to sound that is the hallmark of the book and audio package. Background sound effects, such as thunder moving in before a storm, rain falling, and birds chirping, add to the information presented. In a little more than one hundred words, the topic of rain is introduced with clear enunciation and effective vocal energy. The page-turn rate is also helpful for young listeners. The book includes narration of an appendix of facts about rain that completes the information. This Ready-to-Read series includes *Wind*, *Clouds*, and *Snow*.

STANDARD—SCIENCE
Students will observe weather changes to understand the properties of water change.

Red Sings from Treetops: A Year in Colors,* written by Joyce Sidman, illustrated by Pamela Zagarenski, narrated by Barbara Caruso, Recorded Books

Listeners will be enchanted by the illustrations in this 2010 Caldecott Honor title that turns the annual cycle of seasons into a whimsical combination of poetry, color, and art. From the musical introduction and muted piano background to the light vocal narration, this lovely expression of the season's transitions is a fine example of a read-along that gives the listener time to look at the beautiful folk art and see colors in each season. The free verse is quickly read, with pauses between seasons and highlighting of how colors can be seen in each, from the red of a cardinal in spring to the red of apples in autumn. The narration heightens the poetic word images as the seasons and colors change. An excellent choice for interdisciplinary themes of poetry, science, and art.

STANDARDS—ENGLISH LANGUAGE ARTS, SCIENCE, AND FINE ARTS
Students will read a variety of literature, including poetry; students will become familiar with the cycle of the seasons; students will begin to see the integration between nature and art.

*Rosa,** written and narrated by Nikki Giovanni, illustrated by
Bryan Collier, Weston Woods

The biography of Rosa Parks serves to draw attention to specific benefits of the audiobook read-aloud format. Nikki Giovanni's narration confirms that an author voicing her own words can be a distinct pleasure for listeners, and the luminous illustrations give students the additional visual literacy connection to this story of the civil rights leader. With both music and sound effects, this audiobook package warrants instructional use for curricular themes in African American history and biography.

STANDARD—HISTORY/SOCIAL STUDIES
Students gain knowledge of historical figures and how they helped to shape community, state, and national events.

*Seven Blind Mice,** written and illustrated by Ed Young, narrated
by B. D. Wong, Weston Woods

Something strange is at the pond, and seven variously colored blind mice venture down to explore during the course of a week. One reports that it is "sturdy," and another finds it to be "supple." Each discovers a different attribute in this vocabulary-rich tale, but it is the wise white mouse that sees the whole. Exotic music, squeaky mice, and the measured narration add to the tension in the story. The afterword, read by the author-illustrator, provides insight into his creative process as well as useful advice on classroom applications.

STANDARD—MATHEMATICS
Students can differentiate between defining and nondefining attributes; students can determine measurable attributes of objects.

*Stop Drop and Roll,** written by Margery Cuyler, illustrated by
Arthur Howard, narrated by Ellen Archer, Live Oak Media

Fire Prevention Week generates great angst for Jessica, who worries about everything from making sure her dog has enough water to ensuring (with the help of many alarm clocks) that she gets up in time for school. When her teacher begins talking about fire safety precautions, Jessica's worrying goes into high gear. Archer's deliberate pacing and subtle inflections capture the adults and siblings with their varying degrees of authority, frustration, and humor. Archer makes Jessica wholly believable as a young nervous Nellie. Beginning with lively music and the fears Jessica voices on the jacket flap, and ending with the reading of "Sparky's Top 10 Fire Safety Tips for Kids" from the back of the book jacket, this is a good choice for Fire Prevention Week in all kindergarten and first-grade classes.

STANDARD—HEALTH

Students will identify and explain the need for personal safety behaviors, including fire safety.

That Book Woman, * written by Heather Henson, pictures by
David Small, narrated by Walker Harrison, Weston Woods

Cal, a young boy living in the isolated hills of Appalachia, introduces his story of the horse-riding, persistent woman who brings his family books. His sister Lark is happy for the free loans and devours the stories, but Cal is resistant to "larnin," and he sulks and frowns (with Small's illustrations aptly depicting this solid stubbornness). Harrison's young voice is fittingly country, with a childlike and lilting cadence. Background bluegrass music adds to the atmosphere as Cal is slowly but surely won over by the regular arrival of that book woman! She brings him the fire to learn to read, and Lark is the willing teacher. The story is inspired by the work of the Pack Horse Librarians in Kentucky after the Great Depression.

STANDARD—ENGLISH LANGUAGE ARTS

Students will be able to use strategies to interpret and evaluate a wide range of texts in order to appreciate human experience.

The Treasure, * written and illustrated by Uri Shulevitz, narrated
by Jim Weiss, Live Oak Media

Isaac follows the dream that seems to point him in the direction of finding a treasure, heading off on a long journey to the city. Because he is so poor, the journey is a difficult one, as Isaac must make much of it by foot. Once in the city, a chance encounter with a soldier sends the story to a full-circle conclusion. Weiss's background as a storyteller suits this adaptation of an old English tale, and his measured performance is the ideal complement to Shulevitz's spare text and jewel-like illustrations. This 1980 Caldecott Honor Book is a Common Core text exemplar for grades 2–3.

STANDARD—ENGLISH LANGUAGE ARTS
Students will be able to summarize details of a story including plot, characters, setting, and conclusion.

The True Story of the Three Little Pigs*,* written by Jon Scieszka, illustrated by Lane Smith, narrated by Paul Giamatti, Weston Woods

As in no other version of the three inveterate pigs, the listener can hear Alexander T. Wolf's perspective and what a twist this tale takes. As a read-along, Smith's droll illustrations heighten the absurd, almost sly, retelling of the pigs and their predicament with the wolf. Giamatti's narration has a wry tone and moves the narrative with good pacing and inflection. Even the somewhat innocent nasal tone of the wolf's voice precedes his first great sneeze, and the listener can only smile as the pig's house is blown down. The jaunty background music adds to the satirical comedy and lighthearted atmosphere. This is a natural platform to use with the many variations of the Three Little Pigs story.

STANDARD—ENGLISH LANGUAGE ARTS
Students will listen to traditional literature, including fairy tales and folktales such as the Brothers Grimm and Hans Christian Andersen, in order to compare and contrast themes in various stories.

Truly Winnie, written by Jennifer Jacob Richardson, narrated by Laura Hamilton, Live Oak Media

Winnie goes to camp in this short beginning chapter book. Familiar camp routines such as swimming, chores, crafts, and bunkmates intertwine with themes of friendship, single-parent families, and the dilemma of lying. From the lively introductory music to the multivoiced "chicka chicka boom" cheer, the audio background adds an authentic touch to the story. Hamilton's voice is appropriately young, and she does an excellent job distinguishing individual characters. The chapter breaks and pacing work well to increase the listen-aloud applications of this believable story. Young listeners will also enjoy *Winnie, Dancing on Her Own* and *Winnie at Her Best*.

STANDARD—HISTORY/SOCIAL STUDIES
Students will learn to function in a group by being responsible, trustworthy, respectful, and accountable for their own actions.

What Charlie Heard,* written, illustrated, and narrated by
   Mordecai Gerstein, Live Oak Media

What do composers hear that makes them create their music? A perfect audio interpretation of this picture-book biography of composer Charles Ives answers that question. The inclusion of sound effects and background music allows children to hear, and to see through Gerstein's art, what inspired Ives to write his music. Bits of Ives's compositions combine with a well-paced reading that highlights the author's obvious affection for his subject in this stellar package.

STANDARD—MUSIC
Students understand how and why people respond to their environment through music.

Why Mosquitoes Buzz in People's Ears,* retold by Verna
   Aardema, illustrated by Leo Dillon and Diane Dillon, narrated
   by James Earl Jones, Weston Woods

The listening experience of this 1976 Caldecott Medal–winning tale is a treat, as James Earl Jones brings a West African cadence to his remarkable deep baritone. Authentic background music adds to the story of how mosquitoes became such pests to all living things. The domino effect that the mosquito trips contains a moral—and has listeners wondering whether the sun will shine again. From the iguana to the rabbit, the monkey to the owl, only King Lion can solve the trouble, to the mosquito's chagrin. This is an incomparable read-along that embellishes the iconic illustrations.

STANDARD—ENGLISH LANGUAGE ARTS
Students will be able to retell stories, including fables and folktales from other cultures, and also relate their central message, lesson, or moral.

NOTES
1. Common Core, "English Language Arts Standards: Reading: Foundational Skills: Introduction," www.corestandards.org/the-standards/english-language-arts-standards/reading-foundational-skills/introduction/.
2. Common Core, "Common Core State Standards for English Language Arts and Literacy in History/Social Studies, Science, and Technical Subjects—Appendix B: Text Exemplars and Sample Performance Tasks," www.corestandards.org/assets/Appendix_B.pdf.

5
~
Audiobooks and the Intermediate Primary School

Grades 3–5

*M*oving on to the intermediate grades means the inclusion of more chapter books and longer informational titles. However, wise teachers, librarians, and parents will not overlook the value of picture books, both fiction and nonfiction, for children in grades 3–5. Picture books, particularly for older readers, have rich, complex texts that increase vocabulary, particularly when paired with artwork that affords further opportunities for increasing those important visual literacy skills. The read-along format, as noted in the previous chapter, enhances the development of fluency and correct pronunciation.

Reading comprehension is at the core of the majority of selections in this chapter. Whether through excellent picture-book biographies, tall tales, classics, or an exciting mystery, students will be exposed to a wide variety of literary and informational texts, thus expanding their ability to recognize and discuss a range of content along the appropriate grade-level instructional spectrum. We document text exemplars from the Common Core Standards, and designate read-alongs with an asterisk after the title.

The 100-Year-Old Secret, written by Tracy Barrett, narrated by
David Pittu, Listening Library

Mysteries for young readers are often difficult to find for those genre assignments, so it's especially nice to find a series that is accessible to a wide variety of readers. This first book in the Sherlock Files features twelve-year-old Xena and her ten-year-old brother Xander, recently transplanted from Florida to London with their parents. A mysterious message leads to the discovery that they are direct descendants of the famous detective Sherlock Holmes and heirs to his notebooks and files. Armed with this information, Xena and Xander and their new friends set off to solve a crime that had eluded their celebrated ancestor. Combining themes of a family's move and a new school with the overtones of a classic Sherlock Holmes mystery will surely engage young listeners. Through Pittu's skillful, measured pacing and his ability to switch from American to British English with ease, listeners will not only enjoy a light mystery but also learn some cultural differences between themselves and their cousins across the pond.

STANDARD—ENGLISH LANGUAGE ARTS
Students will read literature across a variety of genres.

Action Jackson,* written by Jan Greenberg and Sandra Jordan,
illustrated by Robert Andrew Parker, narrated by Ed Harris,
Live Oak Media

Documenting the creative process—the making of art—this read-along biography of Jackson Pollock focuses on a two-month period when he painted *Number 1, 1950,* also known as *Lavender Mist.* Dynamic narration, apt sound effects, and musical interludes representing the influence of jazz on his work accentuate the rich, lyrical text that portrays a sometimes reflective, sometimes frenetic technique that culminated in Jackson's controversially "wild" paintings. Parker's India ink and watercolor wash art convey the energy of Pollock's work style while the pacing of the reading and the carefully timed page-turn signals allow students plenty of time to immerse themselves in this remarkable Sibert Honor book.

STANDARD—THE ARTS
Students read biographies of artists and can relate how the artists reflected or influenced the culture of their time.

Alice's Adventures in Wonderland, written by Lewis Carroll, narrated by Jim Dale, Listening Library

Jim Dale, wizard of the fully voiced production, brings his enormous talent to this old and much-loved classic. When the intrepid Alice tumbles down the rabbit hole, she bumps up against the absurd—and vast—population of Wonderland. Dale infuses every denizen of this bizarre world with a unique voice, bringing forth all of the bemused humor inherent in Carroll's text. Fans of the Harry Potter series will be happy to find another outstanding listening experience featuring their favorite narrator. A Common Core text exemplar for grades 4–5.

STANDARD—ENGLISH LANGUAGE ARTS
Students will listen to, read, and discuss complex texts.

Why audiobooks? I'm a convert. The value and evaluation of audiobooks are now included each semester that I teach a survey course in children's literature. Why? It presents a story (whether of fact or fiction) in another way, a different kind of reading perhaps. What did it take for this conversion? Listening, mostly. Listening to more audiobooks to actually hear the difference between the good, the mediocre, and the bad. Listening to the research findings that support the educational uses of audiobooks. Listening contentedly while on endless road trips with my family. Listening to the correct pronunciation of the names and places in favorite fantasies. And listening to Jim Dale read just about anything.

—**Maria Salvadore, children's literature consultant and lecturer,**
University of Maryland, College Park

American Tall Tales, by Mary Pope Osborne, narrated by Scott Snively, Audio Bookshelf

Nine stories featuring some of the astounding characters of American folktales, including Paul Bunyan, John Henry, Pecos Bill, and Johnny Appleseed, are brought to life through Osborne's appealing text and Snively's spot-on narration. Not only is each personality vocally well defined; Snively also manages to imbue his narration with an accurate geographical feeling. Occasional harmonica music rounds out the production, which is a perfect choice for classroom and family listening.

STANDARD—ENGLISH LANGUAGE ARTS
Students will be able to identify characteristics of a tall tale.

Baseball Saved Us,* written and narrated by Ken Mochizuki,
    illustrated by Dom Lee, Live Oak Media

Mochizuki is the perfect narrator for this contemplative look at how baseball made life bearable for Japanese boys in a World War II desert internment camp. Mochizuki reads with gentle determination as Shorty and his campmates resolve to master the game of baseball. When the war is over and Shorty returns home, he is still the brunt of insults, but his baseball prowess helps him find a place with the neighborhood children. Soft background music adds to the pensive nature of the book, leaving the power of Mochizuki's words and narration as well as Lee's brown-toned illustrations to capture listeners' attention. Pair this with *Players in Pigtails* for two very different looks at baseball during World War II.

STANDARD—HISTORY/SOCIAL STUDIES
Students will understand that knowledge of the past helps us to analyze the causes of events and how those events represent the time and place in which they occurred.

***Because of Winn-Dixie**, written by Kate DiCamillo, narrated by
    Cherry Jones, Listening Library

In this 2001 Newbery Honor story, a scruffy dog, found in a grocery store parking lot, becomes the catalyst for ten-year-old Opal to find new friends, learn about her absent mother, and understand that good things often come in unexpected places. Winn-Dixie, aptly named for the grocery store, is the rescued dog that brings comfort to Opal and her father. They both learn to accept the abandonment by Opal's mother, and with Winn-Dixie by her side, Opal discovers for herself what family and friendship mean. Jones, a Tony Award winner and Tennessee native, brings a believable Southern lilt to the reading of this popular short novel. The strong narrative pull engages listeners and showcases an especially effective audiobook.

STANDARD—ENGLISH LANGUAGE ARTS
Students will be able to identify literature with universal themes and apply reading strategies to improve comprehension and fluency.

***The Birchbark House**, written by Louise Erdrich, narrated by
    Nicolle Littrell, Audio Bookshelf

The cycle of the seasons is ever present in the story of Omakayas and her Ojibwa family, who live on an island in Lake Superior in the 1800s. As Omakayas recounts the rhythm of life her people have shared for generations, listeners will come to have a more grounded understanding of what was lost when white settlers moved inexorably westward. Children who have read *The Little House in the Big Woods* will be amazed to hear the other side of the story and to understand the cultural richness of Native American heritage. From planting to harvesting, tanning a moose hide, and the devastation of smallpox, listeners will be entranced by Littrell's storyteller's pacing, which lends itself well to the lyrical text.

STANDARD—HISTORY/SOCIAL STUDIES
Students will explore the culture and history of American Indian tribes and bands.

Blues Journey,* written by Walter Dean Myers, illustrated by
Christopher Myers, narrated by Richard Allen, Live Oak
Media

Soulful poems are paired with remarkable paintings in blue ink and white paint on brown paper bags in this work. Although Myers provides an extensive introduction to the meaning and cadence of the blues, it is the musical underbed and Allen's expressive reading of these call-and-response poems that bring out the passion of the African American experience behind this genre. The book alone is visually and emotionally appealing, but it is the audio that breathes life into it, giving young listeners the necessary musical and narrative accompaniment they need to fully immerse themselves in this astonishing package.

STANDARDS—ENGLISH LANGUAGE ARTS AND MUSIC
Students will explore how multimedia elements affect appreciation of a text; students will listen to and describe music from various cultures.

Bud, Not Buddy, written by Christopher Paul Curtis, narrated by
James Avery, Listening Library

The author writes historical fiction with a unique combination of authentic background information, good characters, and a twist of humor. The 2000 Newbery Medal winner introduces Bud, a ten-year-old African American foster child who flees from Michigan to escape one last unbearable foster home. As listeners follow Bud's journey to find his hoped-for father, narrator Avery brings the boy's hard times, his hope, and his quirky wit to the fore. Even though the Depression-era hardships are not diminished, the characters, especially Bud, shine, which makes this a fine audiobook for classroom and school assignments. Although this is a Common Core text exemplar for grades 2–3, *Bud, Not Buddy* clearly demonstrates how independent listening comprehension can differ. This story fits most solidly into grades 3–5 for listening context and comprehension (for a fuller rationale, see chapter 2).

STANDARD—HISTORY/SOCIAL STUDIES
Students will be able to relate how economics affects people, especially the Depression–era period of U.S. history.

Charlotte's Web, written and narrated by E. B. White, Listening Library

The classic tale about Charlotte, Wilbur, and Fern is, if possible, strengthened by the author's narration. The realities of farm life, the connection between humans and animals, and the strong theme of friendship demonstrate universal appeal. To hear the voice of White heightens the listener's pleasure and showcases the grandfatherly voice of the creator of the well-loved story. As the plot unfolds, listeners surely experience the delight of listening to stories. The author knows the characters, because they are his, and this gives a real and unique power to the words, presenting students with a whole new perspective about storytelling. This 1953 Newbery Honor Book is a Common Core text exemplar for grades 2–3.

STANDARD—ENGLISH LANGUAGE ARTS
Students will describe how the actions of the characters in a story influence the sequence of events.

The Dinosaurs of Waterhouse Hawkins,* written by Barbara Kerley, illustrated by Brian Selznick, narrated by Jonathan Pryce, Weston Woods

This stunning read-along follows the career of Waterhouse Hawkins, a Victorian artist who, working with scientific advisors, was the first to craft three-dimensional figures of newly discovered dinosaurs. The fascinating text is enhanced by a vigorous and authoritative narration, perfectly paced to allow ample time for listeners to explore the 2002 Caldecott Honor paintings that give insight into the ways art and science were intertwined throughout Hawkins's life. Music and sound effects provide a "you are there" component to the triumphs and tragedies of Hawkins's career—from the cheering crowds at the Crystal Palace to Boss Tweed's destructive thugs who kept the dinosaurs from enjoying a home in New York's Central Park. This superb package offers many interdisciplinary opportunities, from science to art, history, and biography.

STANDARD—SCIENCE

Students will use a variety of sources to learn about people who have contributed to major ideas in science.

The Dreamer, written by Pam Muñoz Ryan, illustrated by Peter Sís, narrated by Tony Chiroldes, Scholastic Audio*

From the lyrical prose, to Sís's distinctive illustrations, this fictionalized biography of the Chilean poet Pablo Neruda begins with background music that invites the listener into the story. From early childhood, Neruda listened to a different drummer, and he suffered bullying not only from other children but also from his own father. As he walks through the tropical rain forest, he learns to trust his emerging talent and how poetry can express life's emotions. Chiroldes's authentic accent and rhythmic narration enhance the intertwining of Muñoz Ryan's beautiful prose with Sís's luminous illustrations. The inclusion of an author's endnote and a selection of Neruda's poetry add to this 2011 Pura Belpré Award story.

STANDARD—ENGLISH LANGUAGE ARTS

Students will demonstrate their understanding of the differences between poems, drama, and prose, and be able to describe the elements of poems (e.g., verse, rhythm, meter).

***Encyclopedia Brown Finds the Clues,** written by Donald Sobol, narrated by Greg Steinbruner, Recorded Books*

In 1963, Sobol introduced Leroy Brown, a.k.a. Encyclopedia Brown, a ten-year-old detective who quickly became the go-to mystery series for young readers. Now listeners can enjoy Steinbruner's careful pacing of the simple sentences and appreciate the methodical way that Encyclopedia solves each case. As the sleuth notes the details of each mystery, he helps the Idaville police chief: his dad. The simple chapter format presents a separate case for Encyclopedia to solve, and the narration follows his problem solving with a step-by-step presentation of the facts, one that has kept fans engaged for many years. The audio format lends itself to listening while solving each mystery.

STANDARD—ENGLISH LANGUAGE ARTS

Students will be able to compare and contrast the plots of stories written by the same author about the same characters (i.e., books in a series).

Granny Torrelli Makes Soup, written by Sharon Creech, narrated
   by Donna Murphy, HarperChildren's Audio

This captivating story explores what goes into making good food and good friends, one of whom has a disability. Rosie's best friend, Bailey, has limited eyesight, but that normally doesn't get in the way of the close friendship they've had since they were practically babies. Now that adolescence is approaching, problems sometimes creep in to disrupt their camaraderie. Thank goodness for Rosie's Granny Torrelli, who manages to restore harmony—not only between Rosie and Bailey but also to the entire neighborhood—with her stories, her cooking, and her homespun wisdom. Murphy's appropriately youthful voice carries listeners along from the soup to the pasta. The exuberant reading will have listeners calling out, "Tutto va bene" along with Granny Torrelli.

STANDARD—ENGLISH LANGUAGE ARTS

Students will be able to draw conclusions about character and plot, making connections between previous experiences and reading selections.

Harry Potter and the Sorcerer's Stone, written by J. K. Rowling,
   narrated by Jim Dale, Listening Library

No listing of recommended audiobook titles for young people would be complete without the iconic Harry Potter series. Not only did this series change what children would read (a book of more than seven hundred pages!), the audiobooks changed what children would listen to and sparked a revolution in the audiobook market for children and teens. The seven-volume series opens with abused orphan Harry Potter suffering at the hands of the uncaring aunt, uncle, and cousin with whom he lives. On his eleventh birthday, Harry discovers that he is a wizard and is enrolled in Hogwarts School of Witchcraft and Wizardry, where he meets others with his previously incomprehensible skills. Although the series is wrapped in a cloak of magical feats, it is essentially a long story of the meaning of friendship and love and the battle of good against evil. As the series progresses, and as Harry and his companions age, the themes become darker and are more appropriate for middle and high school students (for an excellent activity for high school students, see chapter 8). Dale's award-winning narration for this series earned him several Grammy and Audie Awards, as well as a 2008 Odyssey Honor. He created 146 distinctive voices over the course of the series. His capacity for flawless pacing not only enhances the tension in the series but also brings out the humor that readers often miss as they speed through the books to discover what happens next. Dale's narration is truly a tour de force.

STANDARD—ENGLISH LANGUAGE ARTS

Students will be able to interpret how an author structures a narrative with details, timing, and pacing that create suspense, tension, or surprise.

The Higher Power of Lucky,
written by Susan Patron, narrated by Cassandra
Campbell, Listening Library

A resourceful ten-year-old, Lucky lives in Hard Pan, California, a place where forty-three residents provide more than enough fodder for this engaging story. The book won the 2007 Newbery Medal. The first page of chapter 1 garnered considerable attention with the use of the word *scrotum*, even though the description—about a dog—was compelling and the scene aptly used the word, but Lucky's story briefly took a back seat to the (unwarranted) controversy! The quirky cast of characters—from her guardian Brigitte to her friends Lincoln and Miles—circle Lucky as she faces the uncertainly of her permanent residence in Hard Pan. The story features wonderful use of language, science themes of desert climate and fauna, the amazing talent of knot tying, and the lure of hidden treasure—with Lucky in the center of it all. Campbell's excellent fully voiced performance gives each character his or her due, from the very young Miles to the French-accented Brigitte. This is the first book in a planned-for trilogy (*Lucky Breaks* in 2009, and *Lucky for Good* in August 2011) and is certainly a fine introduction to Lucky's world.

STANDARD—ENGLISH LANGUAGE ARTS

Students will be able to identify and summarize a story's themes, characters, and plot details.

Igraine the Brave, written by Cornelia Funke, narrated by Xanthe
　　Elbrick, Listening Library

Twelve-year-old Igraine is clever, imaginative, and—yes—bored, but
more important, she wants to break out of the magical family mold and be
a knight: brave, chivalrous, and adventurous. Her opportunity to get that
chance arrives in the form of a quest to bring back a giant's hair—a hair
to undo the magic charm set on her parents, who have been turned into
pigs. From this beginning to a satisfying conclusion, Igraine encounters
more than she expected. The narration by Elbrick includes British accents
that highlight each character and conveys the medieval time, humor, and
fanciful story of Igraine, who truly earns her name, "The Brave."

STANDARD—ENGLISH LANGUAGE ARTS
Students will be able to describe a story's characters, plot and setting in
depth, including the characters' thoughts and actions.

The Journey of the One and Only Declaration of Independence,*
　　written by Judith St. George, illustrated by Will Hillenbrand,
　　narrated by Jeff Brooks, Weston Woods

Surely a manuscript as critical to the inception of the United States has
been vigilantly cared for during all of its existence, right? Wrong! This
amusing account of the extraordinary travels of our seminal national
document—it has "had more homes than a traveling circus"—is
accompanied by lively illustrations that echo the story's wit. Brooks's
robust narrative style fully complements both text and art, with pacing
that allows for time to digest the information and pore over the pictures.
The inclusion of stirring music and sound effects, from crying babies to
cheering crowds and fireworks, creates a read-along experience that's
sure to grab the attention of even the most reluctant young historian.

STANDARD—HISTORY/SOCIAL STUDIES
Students will identify the Declaration of Independence as one of
America's founding documents; students will develop an understanding
of how we learn about the past.

*Knucklehead: Tall Tales and Mostly True Stories about Growing Up
　　Scieszka*, written and narrated by Jon Scieszka, Brilliance Audio

Scieszka obviously delights in this reminiscence of his childhood, and
kids, especially boys, will chuckle right along with him. The second

of six boys, Scieszka recounts many irreverent, often harrowing, but always hilarious adventures with his brothers, friends, and other family members. Although some may wonder at the impudence of Scieszka's shenanigans, particularly those perpetrated against the nuns in his Catholic school, it should be noted that there were always consequences attached to this dubious behavior, and he doesn't shy away from enumerating them. His conversational tone is just right for these episodic, nonsequential stories, and although the book won't work as a read-along, it's certainly a treat for listeners. Pair this with *Math Curse* and *Science Verse* for an interesting author study.

STANDARD—ENGLISH LANGUAGE ARTS
Students will read a variety of nonfiction, including biographies.

Lincoln: A Photobiography, written by Russell Freedman,
    narrated by Robert Petkoff, Listening Library

Russell Freedman, history and biography scholar, won the 1988 Newbery Medal for this groundbreaking format for elementary-age students. Combining extensive period photographs, charts, and facts about the sixteenth president with a strong narrative story brought a fresh view of Lincoln. Can an audiobook overcome the absence of photographs while listening? We give a resounding yes—the compelling and interesting details are narrated by Petkoff, who provides an excellent portrayal of Lincoln and brings an authentic and accurate voice to the biographical facts. This is impeccable storytelling at its best—folksy and concise. The accompanying bonus CD includes author notes and twenty photos, which elevate this engaging audiobook to a higher level. The book is a Common Core text exemplar for grades 2–3.

STANDARD—HISTORY/SOCIAL STUDIES
Students will learn and understand the historical events surrounding the presidency of Abraham Lincoln, including details about his life and times.

Lost! On a Mountain in Maine, written by Donn Fendler,
    narrated by Amon Purinton, Audio Bookshelf

In 1939, when Donn Fendler was twelve years old, he was lost for nine days on Mount Katahdin, the highest peak in Maine. With no food and no shelter, he managed to survive by remembering his Boy Scout skills and relying on his faith in himself, his family, and God. Amon

Purinton was twelve years old when he recorded this audiobook in 1993, which makes for a wonderfully authentic listening experience. His youthful energy and enthusiasm breathe new life into this old story, and he expertly expresses the cold and the hunger and the fear a young boy felt in this terrifying situation. Survival stories are popular, especially with boys; pair this with *A Week in the Woods* for an exciting comparison of a true account and a fictional account of two boys facing similar predicaments.

STANDARD—ENGLISH LANGUAGE ARTS
Students will compare and contrast stories with similar themes or topics.

Love That Dog, written by Sharon Creech, narrated by Scott Wolf, HarperChildren's Audio

Third grader Jack has no use for poetry and resents his teacher's attempts to get him to write his own verses. Initially put off by Robert Frost's "Stopping by Woods on a Snowy Evening," he begins to find poetry interesting and of value when "Mr. Walter Dean Myers" captivates him with "Love That Boy." Jack's move from disdain to admiration and from nonwriter to poet is the stuff of this very short book written in free verse. Wolf completely captures the nuances of third-grade conversation through his pacing and inflection. The flow of the poetry naturally works as a classroom read-aloud, just one reason this works so well as an audiobook. A sequel, *Hate That Cat*, which Wolf also performs, is another fine example of story and poetry, completing Jack's classroom experiences with Miss Stretchberry.

STANDARD—ENGLISH LANGUAGE ARTS
Students listen to fluent spoken language and are able to appreciate various types of literary text, including poetry.

Mack Made Movies,* written and illustrated by Don Brown, narrated by George Guidall, Live Oak Media

This delightful and informative look at Mack Sennett and early movie making is enlivened by whimsical music and sound effects and the dynamic narration of Guidall, who moves the story along at just the right pace. Students will be charmed by Mack, who begins his show-business career as the rear end of a horse and ends it with bringing Charlie

Chaplin and other famous actors to the movie screen. An author's note read by Guidall rounds out a book well suited to discussions of careers, inventions, and the arts.

STANDARD—VISUAL ARTS
Students will be able to understand how visual arts connect with individuals, history, and culture.

---

*The Man Who Walked between the Towers,** written, illustrated, and narrated by Mordicai Gerstein, Live Oak Media

This 2007 Caldecott Medal winner recounts the story of Philippe Petit's 1974 tightrope walk between the twin towers of the World Trade Center in New York City. The poignancy of that memory ignited the author after the destruction of the towers on September 11, and he narrates the story with clarity and pathos. Capturing the world's attention, Petit walked the dizzying heights during the final construction of the towers. He attained notoriety and brief fame with his daring, although his tightrope feat is now only a brief footnote to the past. Gerstein lends his author's voice, with a well-paced and understated reading. Any lesson on the impact of September 11 can be juxtaposed to listening to this compelling story.

STANDARD—ENGLISH LANGUAGE ARTS
Students will be able to describe a text's main events and historical details, including what happened and why.

---

*March On! The Day My Brother Martin Changed the World,** written by Christine King Farris, illustrated by London Ladd, narrated by Lynn Whitfield, Weston Woods

Dr. King's younger sister describes her brother's participation in the 1963 March on Washington, including his writing of the famous "I Have a Dream" speech. Farris's moving account is taken to an even higher emotional level through Whitfield's robust and often passionate narration as she speaks and sings this story. Effective portraits invite readers into this significant event in our history, and an author's note extends the instructional use.

STANDARD—HISTORY/SOCIAL STUDIES
Students will be aware of the struggle for equal rights for all people.

***Math Curse*,** written by Jon Scieszka,
     illustrated by Lane Smith, narrated by Nancy Wu,
     Weston Woods

When Mrs. Fibonacci declares that math applies to every aspect of life, our young protagonist is doomed. Everything does, indeed, reduce itself to a math problem: "I wake up at 7:15. It takes me 10 minutes to get dressed, 15 minutes to eat my breakfast, and 1 minute to brush my teeth . . . if my bus leaves at 8:00, will I make it on time?" Wu serves as the perfect guide through this mathematical nightmare, with inflection that clearly defines characters and pacing that allows listeners to grasp Scieszka's complex and hilarious text as they absorb Smith's busy, object-filled illustrations. Music and sound effects add to the enjoyment of this real, if comical, math lesson.

STANDARD—MATHEMATICS
Students will make use of connections within and outside mathematics to solve mathematical problems.

***No Talking*,** written by Andrew Clements, narrated by Keith
     Nobbs, Simon and Schuster Audio

Laketon Elementary School's fifth-grade class has long been known as the "Un-Shushables" for its inability to ever be quiet. Matters get even worse when war between the sexes breaks out, led by ringleaders Lynsey and Dave, with constant angry shouting back and forth. Then, in one furious moment, Dave challenges the girls to a no-talking-for-forty-eight-hours competition. Their carefully composed rules have parents and teachers baffled and lead to some remarkable results. Nobbs perfectly captures the tone and cadence of early adolescence, making listeners feel that they are right in the Laketon hallways and classrooms.

STANDARD—HISTORY/SOCIAL STUDIES
Students will demonstrate their ability to function as part of a group.

***Odd and the Frost Giants*,** written and narrated by Neil Gaiman,
     HarperChildren's Audio

Odd is an unlucky boy—his father has died, his right leg and foot were crushed, and his mother has remarried a nasty man with too many children. In March of a winter that seems to never end, Odd leaves home and encounters three strange creatures who lead him into an amazing adventure. As always, Gaiman spins an enchanting yarn, and his comfortable narrative style makes for wonderful listening. The musical underbed at the beginning and end of the story adds an appropriate bookend to this short novel based on Norse mythology.

STANDARD—ENGLISH LANGUAGE ARTS
Students will become familiar with characters from culturally diverse mythology, including Greek, Roman, and Norse.

The Phantom Tollbooth, written by Norton Juster, narrated by David Hyde Pierce, HarperChildren's Audio

The first publication date of *The Phantom Tollbooth* was in 1961, so for fifty years children have responded to Milo and the tollbooth that suddenly appears in his room. What adventures he has and what a solution to his lament about being bored! In the hands of the impeccable Pierce, Milo's journey through the tollbooth and into many curious places is a delight. Wordplay, imagination, even math are all put into play with each encounter Milo has, including the Whether Man, the Doldrums, and the Word Market. An interview with the author is included, bringing to conclusion a fine, rollicking story.

STANDARD—ENGLISH LANGUAGE ARTS
Students will be able to determine the meaning of words in a text and differentiate between literal and nonliteral language.

Piper Reed, Navy Brat, written by Kimberly Willis Holt, narrated by Emily Janice Card, Recorded Books

When they're done with Judy Moody and Junie B. Jones, offer up Piper Reed. Made from the same spunky mold as these popular heroines, Piper Reed brings even more to the table. She's a military kid, and in this first book of the series, her family is picking up and moving from San Diego, California, to Pensacola, Florida (where her dad will be shipping out for six months)—after the school year has already started! This is tough going for a middle child with dyslexia, but Piper rises to the challenge with plenty of help from family and new friends. Card's peppy narration is perfectly suited to Piper's energy and enthusiastic outlook and brings additional vigor to an already engaging story.

STANDARD—HISTORY/SOCIAL STUDIES
Students will demonstrate the ability to interact within a group, performing various group roles including organizing, planning, and goal setting.

***Players in Pigtails*,** written by Shana Corey, illustrated
    by Rebecca Gibbon, narrated by Zooey Deschanel,
    Weston Woods

Baseball-loving students may be surprised to discover that there was
once the All-American Girls Professional Baseball League. How the
league came to be unfolds through the story of Katie Casey, a girl who
loved baseball more than anything but who was not allowed to play:
"What good is baseball to a girl?" When World War II disrupted the
professional men's leagues, Phillip Wrigley started a league for girls so
Americans could continue to enjoy their national pastime. This lively
text with accompanying watercolor and colored-pencil illustrations
reminiscent of primitive folk art are further enhanced by Deschanel's
forthright, energetic narration over a musical bed of ball-park music
and sound effects. Use this for Women's History Month, units on how
World War II affected the home front, or to celebrate the opening of the
baseball season.

> **STANDARD—HISTORY/SOCIAL STUDIES**
> Students will study how an individual develops a personal identity by
> exploring the influence of people, places, and events on their personal
> development, including setting personal goals, and developing
> understanding of others.

***The Problem with the Puddles*,** written by Kate Feiffer,
    narrated by Halley Feiffer, Listening Library

Mr. and Mrs. Puddle can't agree on anything—not even the name of
their daughter. When they leave the country to return to the city, their
dogs Big Sally and Little Sally are accidentally left behind, setting the
stage for some hilarious misadventures and a surprise reunion. Halley
Feiffer captures the silliness and sarcasm with her vocalizations of the
outrageous characters in this middle-grade novel. She's especially good
at the interplay between Big Sally and Little Sally. There are lots of
funny moments here, and students will appreciate the clever plot twists
while they attempt to predict the outcome of this very silly story.

> **STANDARD—ENGLISH LANGUAGE ARTS**
> Students will describe characters in a story and explain how their
> behavior drives the action and sequence of events.

Ramona the Pest, written by Beverly Cleary,
    narrated by Stockard Channing,
    Listening Library

Known to her legion of fans, Ramona Quimby is now off to kindergarten, where she finds that her energetic enthusiasm is challenging to her teacher and classmates. A classmate's bouncy curls captivate her, and she has difficulty with being "quiet." Troubles ensue, as always, but Ramona's charm brings a happy ending. Stockard Channing *is* Ramona as she uses her voice and pacing to create a girl that has humor and spunk. This chapter book has endured because of the universal themes of family, school, and growing up

> **STANDARD—ENGLISH LANGUAGE ARTS**
> Students will be able to compare and contrast the plots and themes of books by the same author about the same character or characters (i.e., books in a series).

Reaching for the Moon,* written and narrated
    by Buzz Aldrin, illustrated by Wendell Minor,
    Live Oak Media

Aldrin tells the story of his life, with special emphasis on his historic trip aboard *Apollo 11* to become one of the first two people on the moon. From his boyhood passions for flight and rock collecting, everything seems to have guided Aldrin to his participation in that first moon landing, during which his job was to collect moon rocks. With quiet composure and a sturdy pacing, Aldrin tells his story, allowing plenty of time for listeners to pore over Minor's meticulous paintings. His narration is accompanied by music and sound effects that include parts of the actual NASA recordings from that historic voyage, including the famous "The Eagle has landed" and Neil Armstrong's "One small step for man; one giant leap for mankind."

> **STANDARD—SCIENCE**
> Students will observe and explain changes to objects in the sky, including the sun and the moon; students will construct models representing Earth, the sun, and the moon and their orbital relationships to one another.

Sarah, Plain and Tall, written by Patricia MacLachlan, narrated
　　by Glenn Close, Harper Children's Audio

The recipe for a fine audiobook calls for one part well-written and
compelling story, one part exceptional narration, which is then mixed
with a number of instructional themes. *Sarah, Plain and Tall* combines
all these ingredients for a very satisfying listening experience. Sarah
travels from Maine to Kansas in response to Jacob's ad for a wife and
mother to Anna and Caleb, his motherless children. Anna narrates the
story as Sarah adjusts to prairie life while missing the ocean vistas
of Maine. Set in the early 1900s, the story's expressive language is
beautifully performed by Close, who creates individual voices that distill
each character. The 1986 Newbery Medal novel is also a Common Core
text exemplar for grades 2–3.

STANDARD—ENGLISH LANGUAGE ARTS
Students will be able to retell a story, describing plot details, and how
characters respond to events and challenges.

Science Verse,* written by Jon Scieszka, illustrated by Lane
　　Smith, narrated by the author and illustrator and various
　　children, Viking

In a companion volume to *Math Curse*, Mr. Newton proclaims: "You
know, if you listen closely enough, you can hear the poetry of science
in everything." Uh-oh, our poor boy now hears poetry in every science
lesson. Smith's collage art, wholly incorporated with the text, adds color
and dimension. Although this is not technically a read-along, Scieszka
and Smith are at their uproarious best reading and "discussing" the
poems, making connections to the parodied originals. Unidentified
children delightfully sing several poems. There is real science to be
learned here—if you can stop laughing.

STANDARD—ENGLISH LANGUAGE ARTS
Students will be able to recognize and explain how word choices help
develop mood and meaning in poetry.

Snowflake Bentley,* written by Jacqueline Briggs Martin, illustrated
　　by Mary Azarian, narrated by Sean Astin, Weston Woods

Wilson Bentley grew up on a farm in Jericho, Vermont, where, at an
early age, he became fascinated by snowflakes. The story of Bentley's

remarkable discovery—that no two snowflakes are alike—is told in this picture-book biography through graceful, multilayered text and luminous, 1999 Caldecott Medal–winning woodblock illustrations. Astin's measured pace is well suited to the structure of the book, which can be enjoyed with or without reading the informational sidebars. The same choice is possible in the audio edition; track 1 (with page-turn signals) and track 3 (without page-turn signals) are read without including the sidebar information, whereas tracks 2 and 4 include the reading of the sidebars.

STANDARD—ENGLISH LANGUAGE ARTS
Students will read to acquire information and will be able to connect new information to prior knowledge.

Stop the Train! written by Geraldine McCaughrean, narrated by
Ellen Myrick and the Full Cast Family, Full Cast Audio

Historical fiction can be both informative and entertaining, and this story fits both categories. From the tongue-twister name of young Cissy Sissney to the quirky cast of characters, this tale has a unique point of view, the building of the railroads. Oklahoma is where Cissy and her family settle, brought there by a train, literally to the "middle of nowhere." Set in the early 1890s and based on a true story of the Oklahoma land rush, these settlers faced adversity while trying to carve out a life in which hardship was a daily presence. Once the railroad decides to bypass their little town, the fun begins as the community devises ways to keep the town alive. A full cast of narrators, including children, highlights the humor and wonderful use of language. Add the original musical score and listeners will feel a tangible connection to the Old West.

STANDARD—HISTORY/SOCIAL STUDIES
Students will learn about the U.S. westward expansion, including the importance of building the railroads and the role of the settlers.

Tales from the Odyssey Audio Collection, written by Mary Pope
Osborne, narrated by James Simmons, HarperChildren's Audio

Osborne's considerable flair for writing engaging historical narrative is paired with Simmons's incomparable vocal talents to make these stories— *The One-Eyed Giant, The Land of the Dead, Sirens and Sea Monsters,*

The Grey-Eyed Goddess, Return to Ithaca, and *The Final Battle*—come alive for readers in a whole new way. From the monstrous Cyclops to the heroic Odysseus, Simmons creates distinctive portrayals of the larger-than-life characters that populated Greek mythology. This not only lends itself to classroom use but also is a great choice for family listening. *The One-Eyed Giant* is a Common Core text exemplar for grades 2–3.

STANDARD—ENGLISH LANGUAGE ARTS
Students will be able to identify significant characters in Greek mythology.

Trumpet of the Swan, written and narrated by E. B. White,
Listening Library

The classic story of Louis, the cygnet who struggles to trumpet, will charm a new generation of listeners with this impeccable reading by the author. The fanciful story, a variation on the theme of finding one's voice, is further enhanced by hearing the voice of White, and who can improve on that? The inclusion of sound effects, science facts, and learning to overcome obstacles only improves the instructional themes in this excellent audiobook production.

STANDARD—ENGLISH LANGUAGE ARTS
Students will be able to describe characters in a story and explain the sequence of events to understand plot structure.

We Are the Ship: The Story of Negro League Baseball, written by
Kadir Nelson, narrated by Dion Graham, Brilliance Audio

Nelson's everyman narrator is embodied in the voice of Graham, whose mellow baritone invites listeners into the dugout and onto the field with the stars of the Negro Leagues. From the misery of rampant racism to the exhilaration of a game well played, this parallel history of America's pastime comes to life. The outstanding paintings that ran through the book are available on an accompanying CD. A blues harmonica introduces and ends the story, and an interview with the author completes this stellar package, which is not only a Common Core text exemplar for grades 4–5 but also the winner of multiple awards: the 2009 Coretta Scott King Author Award and Illustrator Honor, the 2009 Robert F. Sibert Informational Book Medal, and a 2010 Odyssey Honor.

STANDARD—ENGLISH LANGUAGE ARTS
Students will read and listen to gain information and understanding.

A Week in the Woods, written by Andrew Clements, narrated by
    Ron Livingston, Listening Library

Mark Chelmsley IV is a wealthy and spoiled only child. When his parents move the family from suburban New York City to a farmhouse in New Hampshire, Mark determines that he will not assimilate to rural life. Blind to his feelings of loss, science teacher Mr. Maxwell is quick to misjudge Mark, sending him packing from the class camping trip. Not surprisingly, they end up in the woods dependent on each other for survival. Livingston's inflection and pacing match the tempos of action-filled as well as reflective scenes. He manages the interior monologues of both Mark and Mr. Maxwell with the same energy and expression he brings to the rest of the story, which allows listeners to gain understanding of both characters. As mentioned previously, this book works well in combination with another survival story, *Lost! On a Mountain in Maine*, for lessons on the comparison of differing views of similar topics.

STANDARD—ENGLISH LANGUAGE ARTS
Students will examine different approaches to accounts of related topics, noting similarities as well as differences.

What to Do about Alice? How Alice Roosevelt Broke the Rules,
*Charmed the World, and Drove Her Father Teddy Crazy,**
    written by Barbara Kerley, illustrated by Edwin Fotheringham,
    narrated by Katherine Kellgren, Weston Woods

President Theodore Roosevelt once declared: "I can be president of the United States, or I can control Alice. I cannot possibly do both!" His daughter Alice was a girl who "ate up the world," and her vivacious personality and boundless curiosity come through strongly in this lively read-along. Kerley's recounting of Alice's many escapades is delightfully supported by Fotheringham's whimsically energetic illustrations. The text is chock full of marvelous vocabulary words, such as *gamboled*, *voracious*, and *shriveled*. The often-fanciful font design accentuates important words and phrases. Kellgren manages to bring this all together with pacing and inflection that take full advantage of the excitement, vexation, and adoration that Alice Roosevelt provoked and provided. Kellgren eagerly rushes along or calmly draws out Kerley's text to perfection, making sure that the important words and phrases are given proper importance with her voice. This is an excellent introduction to an overlooked woman in our history and is a fine choice for biography units, especially during Women's History Month.

STANDARDS—ENGLISH LANGUAGE ARTS AND HISTORY/SOCIAL STUDIES
Students will be able to determine the meaning of words used in a story, both literal and nonliteral language; to gain essential skills, students will use a variety of materials such as biographies and folktales.

When Marian Sang,* written by Pam Muñoz Ryan, illustrated by Brian Selznick, narrated by Gail Nelson, Live Oak Media

This lovely read-along biography of the great singer Marian Anderson is a must-listen—from the incandescent illustrations to the musical excerpts and life story of the gifted musician. The audio production lifts the 2003 Robert Sibert Honor book to a new level, describing Marian's rise from the church services in South Philadelphia to the world stages, culminating in the most famous of all, the Easter Sunday concert in 1939 at the Lincoln Memorial. The narration flows as well as the music, and listeners will have the privilege of hearing the voice that stirred thousands of people during her long career that spanned from segregation through the civil rights movement. When Marian sang, the world listened, and so can children today through audio productions such as this.

STANDARD—HISTORY/SOCIAL STUDIES
Students will recognize and respond to famous musicians and artists whose contributions are an integral part of U.S. history.

Where the Mountain Meets the Moon, written by Grace Lin, narrated by Janet Song, Listening Library

In the shadow of Fruitless Mountain, Minli and her parents struggle to make ends meet, barely having enough to eat. When Minli spends one of her last two coins on a goldfish purported to have magical properties, her bitter mother rails against the foolishness put into the girl's head by her tale-spinning father. But Minli believes in those tales and sets out to find the elusive Old Man of the Moon, aided by the fish (who truly is magical) and a dragon. Along the way, Minli encounters danger, friendship, and wisdom—and in the end, she saves the fortunes of her family and her village. Song wraps this enchanting story with the suggestion of Chinese inflection and cadence, adding to the authentic feel of this original folktale. The book is a Common Core text exemplar for grades 4–5.

STANDARD—ENGLISH LANGUAGE ARTS
Students will read and listen to a variety of literary styles and genres.

6

Audiobooks and Middle School

Grades 6–8

*A*s young people enter middle school, their transition to adolescence also marks a change in listening habits. Having a larger role in activities, both in and outside of school, makes students turn to the mobile connections of iPods, MP3 players, and smartphones. The listening connects them to audiobook titles that can fulfill school assignments for English language arts, history and social studies, and science. The choices in this chapter clearly target many instructional themes, but they do not overlook the excellent stories for this age group. Mystery, historical fiction, science, biography, poetry, and fantasy are all represented, including classics and recent award-winning audiobooks.

The Adventures of Huckleberry Finn, written by Mark Twain, narrated by Tom Parker, Blackstone Audiobooks

Parker serves as storyteller in this brilliant production of Twain's classic, much-debated novel of life along the Mississippi. Part of many middle school reading lists, but difficult reading for many, the audiobook format eases the path of understanding and interpreting this wide-ranging look at racism, greed, corruption, slavery, and friendship. Twain's many dialects become comprehensible through Parker's clear, mellifluous tones. His measured pace is the perfect foil to the madcap and dangerous goings-on of the novel. This is an uncensored production of Twain's original work, and it must be said that the use of the *N* word is startling and disturbing. It does, however, offer an excellent starting place for classroom and family discussions on the power of words, as well as how people treat one another.

STANDARD—ENGLISH LANGUAGE ARTS
Students will understand and describe the ways in which authors use characters, conflict, point of view, and tone to build meaning.

My son would have never made it through *Huckleberry Finn* in middle school without listening to it. That is such a tough text for any reader, almost an impossible text for a not-so-confident or struggling reader. The dialects, the pacing of the action, the sentence constructions . . . are from a different time. A *Huckleberry Finn* reader has to be a linguist, an archeologist, and a code-cracker. Listening to the story keeps the story alive.

—Jon Scieszka, children's book author and
2008 Library of Congress Ambassador
for Young People's Literature

Alchemy and Meggy Swann, written by Karen
Cushman, narrated by Katherine Kellgren,
Listening Library

Newbery-winning author Cushman (*The Midwife's Apprentice* and *Catherine, Called Birdy*) has created a tale from Elizabethan London, this one featuring Meggy, a young girl whose strength and courage are tested as she begins a new life with a father who doesn't necessarily want to cope with her or her crippled leg. But perseverance prevails with Meggy's will to adjust, make friends, and win a place in her father's life. Kellgren creates a hearty voice for Meggy, dramatically invoking her archaic epithets with girlish enthusiasm and gritty determination. Background medieval music and Kellgren's British accent add authentic touches to this 2011 Odyssey Honor story of life in another time.

STANDARD—ENGLISH LANGUAGE ARTS
Students will be able to interpret words and phrases used in a text, including figurative speech and how specific words can shape the meaning of a text.

Anne Frank Remembered, written by Miep Gies, narrated by
Barbara Rosenblat, Oasis Audio (Springwater)

A fascinating and gripping memoir that presents the recollections of Miep Gies, who, at the age of almost one hundred, updates her memories of the concealment of Anne Frank and her family during World War II. Gies's background and perception of the Anne Frank story make this an excellent companion to the famous *Diary of a Young Girl*. The description of life in Amsterdam both before and during the Nazi occupation presents details about the Franks and their time in the annex. From the prologue in which Gies describes how many Dutch citizens hid Jews during the war to the day the Franks were taken away to the concentration camps, an excellent performance heightens this memoir. The award-winning narrator, Barbara Rosenblat, paces the narrative with a slightly accented lilt that adds historic authenticity. Overall, the story of the Frank family is given an important perspective through this memoir of the woman who tried her best to save them.

STANDARD—HISTORY/SOCIAL STUDIES
Students will learn and understand historical events and perspective through personal memoir.

Bat 6, written by Virginia Euwer Wolf, narrated by a full cast,
Listening Library

This tragic story of the effects of unchecked prejudice in the aftermath of World War II is told in twenty-one different voices. At the fiftieth anniversary Bat 6 game—the annual girls' softball competition between Barlow and Bear Creek Ridge—two teams take the field in rural Oregon three years after the end of the war, when Japanese neighbors have returned from the internment camps. Each of the young team members relates the events of that fateful spring, creating a masterful whole from the many angles. The audiobook, read by ten narrators who give a distinctive voice to each girl, allows listeners to concentrate on the arc of the story without having to visually navigate the multiple points of view—a difficult task for proficient readers and often impossible for those who struggle to read. This is a particularly good example of how an audiobook production makes print material accessible to a wider audience.

STANDARD—ENGLISH LANGUAGE ARTS
Students will be able to explain the ways in which an author develops and contrasts multiple points of view among characters in a text.

The Beautiful Stories of Life, written by Cynthia Rylant, narrated
    by Alyssa Bresnahan, Recorded Books

Rylant retells six Greek myths—Pandora, Persephone, Orpheus, Pygmalion, Narcissus, and Psyche—in simple and elegant language. She adds her own distinctive details to the stories, thereby making them more personal and accessible to listeners. Bresnahan's measured pacing and formal tone is in keeping with the omniscient narrator Rylant uses in the telling of these universal tales of courage and cowardice, love and loss, which allows the rich vocabulary and the drama of the text to take center stage.

STANDARD—HISTORY/SOCIAL STUDIES
Students will understand the symbolism in Greek mythology; students will understand how the ancient Greeks explained natural events; students will understand how Greek culture influenced the culture of the Western world.

Charles and Emma: The Darwins' Leap of Faith, written by Deborah
    Heiligman, narrated by Rosalyn Landor, Listening Library

The story features the courtship and marriage of Charles and Emma Darwin, from Charles's list of "marry" or "not marry" through the difficulties of their differences in belief about science and religion. The Darwin's had a wonderful, loving marriage despite ill health and the death of several children. They left a legacy of letters and other writings used extensively in this book to shed light on their lives and their relationship. Charles Darwin's scientific work is always at the forefront of both the marriage and Heiligman's text, which Landor gracefully executes with her precise diction and Victorian-sounding voice. Subtle changes in inflection and pacing distinguish the characters is this 2010 Michael L. Printz Honor Book for Excellence in Young Adult Literature that will suit units on scientific inquiry, Victorian life, and the lost art of letter writing.

STANDARD—SCIENCE
Students will understand the process of scientific inquiry to investigate questions, conduct experiments, and solve problems.

Claudette Colvin: Twice toward Justice, written by Phillip Hoose,
    narrated by Channie Waites, Brilliance Audio

Middle school students, with their heightened sense of social justice, will be drawn to this story of the teenager who was arrested for refusing to give up her seat on a Birmingham bus nine months before Rosa Parks's famous act of civil disobedience. Colvin, an upstanding, churchgoing girl, rails against the injustice of Jim Crow laws in the South, and once she decides to pursue resistance, her life becomes increasingly difficult. She is ridiculed and reviled by both white and black communities and falls prey to a smooth-talking older man who leaves her dejected and pregnant. Waites narrates this multilayered piece of nonfiction with aplomb, employing different styles and voices for historical information, including extensive and enlightening sidebars, as well as the many famous names of the civil rights movement, especially Parks and Dr. Martin Luther King Jr. Waites is at her best, however, when giving voice to Colvin herself—through Hoose's extensive interviews. This is a revealing and moving slice of American history made more immediate and accessible through Waites's expert narration. Winner of multiple awards and honors, including the 2009 National Book Award for Young People's Literature, a 2009 Newbery Honor, and a 2009 Robert F. Sibert Informational Book Honor.

STANDARD—HISTORY/SOCIAL STUDIES
Students will examine the civil rights movement and show relationship between civic participation and the attainment of civic goals.

Colibrí, written by Ann Cameron, narrated by Jacqueline Kim, Listening Library

Rosa trudges the back roads of Guatemala with the superstitious, scheming, dishonest "Uncle," who claims to have saved her when she was taken from her parents years ago. Cameron vividly describes Rosa's desperation to reclaim her lost name: Tzunún Chumil ("Hummingbird Star" or "Colibrí," in Spanish) and the honest life that goes with that name. Kim reads with heartbreaking authenticity, drawing the listeners into the story so that they smell the tortillas and beans and feel the dust of the road. Her quiet narration is perfectly suited to the emerging awareness of Tzunún as an honest, brave, and worthwhile young woman.

STANDARD—ENGLISH LANGUAGE ARTS
Students will compare characteristics of culture through language, literature, the arts, institutions, and traditions.

Crows and Cards, written by Joseph Helgerson, narrated by
    MacLeod Andrews, Brilliance Audio

Twelve-year-old Zebulon Crabtree is sent off by riverboat to apprentice
to his great-uncle, a tanner. Zeb really wants a different kind of life
for himself and easily falls under the spell of Chilly Larpenteur, an
unscrupulous gambler. Believing at first that they're helping orphans by
ridding rich men of their money, Zeb soon learns that he's participating
in a cheating card ring. Zeb's escapades include an Indian chief and
his daughter, a wise slave, and a host of other colorful characters in
a story reminiscent of tales by Mark Twain or Bret Harte. Engaging
music, wholly appropriate to the time period, begins and ends each disc.
Andrews employs the ideal voicing and accents for this story, managing
to draw on the highs and lows of Zeb's emotional range from terrified
to excited to disappointed. Other characters are also wholly delineated:
when they are matter of fact, so is Andrews, and when they are over
the top, he is pitch perfect there as well. Reading aloud the dictionary
found at the end of the print edition will not connect with readers, but
it is easily skipped and will not diminish listeners' enjoyment of an
otherwise ripsnortin' tale.

STANDARD—ENGLISH LANGUAGE ARTS
Students will describe elements of character development, setting,
plot, theme, and conflict.

The Dark Is Rising, written by Susan Cooper, narrated by Alex
    Jennings, Listening Library

Cooper's rich language and deeply layered atmosphere combine with
the sumptuous voice of the consummate narrator to further enhance the
experience of reading this 1974 Newbery Honor Book. There are strange
goings-on in Will Stanton's village, from the bizarre behavior of the
rooks to the appearance of the peculiar tramp to the icy cold suddenly
enveloping the area. But strangest of all is the discovery, on his eleventh
birthday, that as one of the Old Ones, he is destined to use heretofore-
unknown magical powers to stave off the Dark that threatens to cover
the world. Jennings's nuanced performance breathes life into each
character as he moves effortlessly from Will's bewildered adolescence
to the honeyed evil that personifies the voice of the Rider. A Common
Core text exemplar for grades 6–8.

Dave at Night, written by Gail Carson Levine, narrated by Jason Harris, Listening Library

The scene is New York City, 1926, and the protagonist, eleven-year-old Dave, tells his story—his father's unexpected death, his being placed in the Hebrew Home for Boys, and his discovery of the music and nightlife of the Harlem Renaissance. Escaping from the terrible food, the bullies, and the strict rules, Dave, in nightly forays outside the orphanage, finds solace in new friends and new opportunities. The narration is partially voiced, with Harris differentiating some characters through pacing and inflection, and others with a distinct voice. The result is an introduction to the artistic heyday of Harlem that is also a wonderful choice for a read-aloud.

The Death-Defying Pepper Roux, written by Geraldine McCaughrean, narrated by Anton Lesser, Listening Library

Conjure up a trio—Harry Potter, Captain Jack Sparrow from *Pirates of the Caribbean*, and Pepper Roux—and there is surely a death-defying romp in store for the listener. Foretold (cursed) to die at the age of fourteen, Pepper escapes his fate by embarking on a succession of nonstop misadventures. As his father is a sea captain, all things nautical, from pirates to knots, are in Pepper's background as he flees his home to seek his real place in the world. McCaughrean's narrative is strengthened by Lesser's performance, from a young-sounding Pepper to his protector-in-disguise Duchesse, the accents hearken to mid-twentieth-century France and beyond. This is an enjoyable tale that demonstrates a tight plot, is well written, and features memorable characters.

Elijah of Buxton, written by Christopher Paul Curtis, narrated by Mirron Willis, Listening Library

Based on true events set in 1859, this is award-winning historical fiction (2008 Newbery Honor, 2008 Coretta Scott King Author Award, and 2009 Odyssey Honor). Elijah Freeman is eleven years old when this fast-paced story opens, with Willis demonstrating a talented interpretation of Elijah and the cast of characters. Elijah's personality is evident as he describes his being the first born in Buxton, the Canadian town founded by runaway slaves. The town faces uncertainties, daily struggles, and even some treachery as Elijah grows to understand how he is connected to his family and community. With twists of humor and pathos, Willis channels Elijah with cultural authenticity and a stellar performance. Don't miss the afterword by the author, who gives an eloquent description of the history of the Buxton settlement.

STANDARD—HISTORY/SOCIAL STUDIES
Students will learn about the settlement, pre–Civil War, of African Americans in Canada gaining their freedom and escaping from slavery.

Esperanza Rising, written by Pam Muñoz Ryan, narrated by Trini Alvarez, Listening Library

Esperanza, almost thirteen, lives a life of privilege in Mexico, but sudden tragedy forces her and her mother to leave their home and escape to California. Set in 1930, migrant farm work mixes with magical realism as Esperanza's story brings her to a life of hard work and poverty. Leaving her former life of comfort behind brings radical changes as Esperanza learns survival skills as she grows to understand the underside of social class, Depression-era deprivation, and even hope for the future. The reader's lilting voice perfectly translates the Spanish words, phrases, and traditions, and those listeners who would struggle with these unfamiliar Spanish names and words will enjoy the audiobook with little effort.

STANDARD—HISTORY/SOCIAL STUDIES
Students will study the roles of people in society, including class structures, family life, and social impact of economic pressures.

The Evolution of Calpurnia Tate, written by Jacqueline Kelly,
    narrated by Natalie Ross, Brilliance Audio

Eleven-year-old Calpurnia struggles against the expectations of a
young lady in 1899 rural Texas. She spurns her mother's attempts to
domesticate her and longs for the freedoms afforded her six brothers.
A budding naturalist, Callie bonds with her unconventional grandfather
who teaches her how to think like a scientist. He lends her a copy of
Darwin's *On the Origin of Species*, and each chapter begins with a
passage from that book, allowing listeners the opportunity to discover
Darwinian theory along with Callie. Her growth, both as a scientist
and as a young woman, is encapsulated in Ross's lively narration, so
well suited to the spirited girl at the center of this story. Pair this 2010
Newbery Honor Book with *Charles and Emma: The Darwins' Leap of
Faith* for interesting classroom comparisons.

STANDARD—ENGLISH LANGUAGE ARTS
Students will compare and contrast a variety of fiction and narrative
nonfiction.

Extra Credit, written by Andrew Clements, narrated by Gabra
    Zachman, Simon and Schuster Audio

Faced with having to repeat sixth grade, Abby Carson agrees to an
extra-credit project—writing to and reporting on a pen-pal exchange
with a young Afghan girl. When she discovers that it is really the girl's
brother, Sadeed, who is the correspondent, the project becomes more
interesting. Their letters provide an engaging format to describe the
commonalities and differences between the two countries. From the
opening Middle Eastern music to Zachman's fully voiced performance,
the alternating chapters between Abby and Sadeed include subtle
cadence and vocal pitch changes. Overall, this is a listening experience
that will engage middle school students with accurate descriptions of
school life. The topical subject of today's Afghanistan is a layer that
should appeal.

STANDARD—HISTORY/SOCIAL STUDIES
Students will gain understanding of people, countries, and cultures
around the world.

Good Masters! Sweet Ladies! Voices from a Medieval Village,
written by Laura Amy Schlitz, narrated by Christina Moore
and a full cast, Recorded Books

Drama is created to be performed, and performance is the hallmark of this audiobook, including medieval music that sets the stage. The 2008 Newbery Medal winner excels in audio, the full-cast format highlighting each character. Monologues capture medieval life and present a cross-section of village roles, from blacksmith to manor heir, and how they intertwine in their daily lives. All the narrators take the proverbial stage and present a memorable play. A wonderful example of an audiobook enhancing the print version, *Good Masters! Sweet Ladies!* will draw listeners who otherwise would miss a special story.

STANDARD—HISTORY/SOCIAL STUDIES
Students will be able to describe medieval manor life with references to specific positions that represent social class and responsibilities.

Graceling, written by Kristin Cashore, narrated by David Baker
and the Full Cast Family, Full Cast Audio

Katsa and Po, two of a special group of people who are graced with horrifying and dangerous special abilities, set out to uncover the answer behind a political mystery and discover themselves in the process. Chelsea Mixon, as Katsa, and Zachary Exton, as Po, are wonderfully believable as the confused and love-torn "gracelings," and the voices of the minor characters are also well developed. Baker's pleasant baritone voice provides the right touch as the narrator. Each disc concludes at just the right spot in the narrative and, like a good cliffhanger chapter ending, spurs the listener on to the next disc, which makes this an excellent choice for group listening.

STANDARD—ENGLISH LANGUAGE ARTS
Students will analyze how an author develops the plot in a text and how a narrator or speaker presents various characters and their different points of view.

The Graveyard Book, written and narrated by Neil Gaiman,
Harper Children's Audio

A thoroughly winning combination—eloquent author, gripping plot, and the pleasure of the author's narration—brings to the listener the story of Nobody, or "Bod." Bod's predicament of living in a graveyard is precipitated by the murder of his parents and sister. Although desperate, Bod's situation is softened by the gentle presence of his protectors, the ghosts of the cemetery. From Gaiman's perfect voicing to creepy background music, this is one audiobook that transcends the 2009 Newbery Medal–winning print version. Gaiman's chilling description of the murderer's continued hunt for Bod is tempered by the kindly care of his ghostly family. Through the terror and suspense of Bod's predicament, the story's expressive language will have listeners asking for more.

STANDARD—ENGLISH LANGUAGE ARTS

Students will be able to compare and contrast reading a story with listening to a story, to measure what they "see" against what they "hear."

The Great Fire, written by Jim Murphy, narrated by Taylor Mali, Audio Bookshelf

On a warm Sunday evening in October 1871, a small fire started that was eventually to leave one hundred thousand Chicago residents homeless and hundreds dead. The Great Chicago Fire burned the city, constructed almost entirely of wood, to the ground as a result of miscommunication and panic. Heroes, victims, and villains were all in plentiful supply, and Murphy tells their stories with impeccable research and historical details. Mali's dynamic baritone voice is ideal for conveying the drama to listeners. Although the numerous photos are not essential to an appreciation of the text, the maps are integral to comprehending the path and speed of the fire. However, listeners who keep a copy of the print edition nearby will be able to follow the fire's route with ease. In fact, for less experienced or struggling readers, the audiobook and print approach will be highly beneficial to a more thorough understanding of the book. This 1996 Newbery Honor Book is also a Common Core text exemplar for grades 6–8.

STANDARD—ENGLISH LANGUAGE ARTS

Students will describe the author's purpose in writing a text and how the author's point of view may differ from that of others.

Hana's Suitcase, written by Karen Levine, narrated by Stephanie Wolfe, Brilliance Audio

An historical artifact, a mystery, and a journey from Tokyo to Canada to Germany drives this unforgettable true story about a Holocaust victim and revelations discovered fifty years after World War II. The year is 2000, and a small suitcase arrives at a Holocaust center in Tokyo—the name on the suitcase is Hana Brady. Who was she? Why does the suitcase just give her name, a date, and a word in German: *orphan*? From these small clues, a Japanese curator searches for and finds the answers to Hana's fate. Wolfe reads with a dispassion that leaves the emotional impact of this story intact, and the interview at the end brings the story to a conclusion that is both uplifting and poignant.

STANDARD—HISTORY/SOCIAL STUDIES
Students will understand and be able to describe the political, economic, social, and personal impact of the Holocaust.

Hoot, written by Carl Hiaasen, narrated by Chad Lowe,
Listening Library

Themes of honesty, ecology, dealing with bullies, child abuse, and making new friends are explored in this mystery that will be particularly appealing to boys. Roy is new to Trace Middle School in Florida, struggling to avoid being victimized and intrigued when he sees a strange boy running by. Splashed with adolescent humor, the 2003 Newbery Honor story pits the endangered burrowing owl against Mother Paula's All-American Pancake House, and the results are a winning combination. The narration by Chad Lowe is unvoiced, but the understated reading manages to bring out the humor of the story. A natural pairing with Hiaasen's *Flush* and *Scat*, the topics of environmental responsibility, protection of wildlife, and animal habitats are explored and provide good background information for science studies.

STANDARD—SCIENCE
Students will learn about environmental threats, food sources, and habitats of various species.

I, Too, Sing America: Three Centuries of African American
Poetry, edited by Catherine Clinton, narrated by Ashley Bryan
and Renee Joshua-Porter, Audio Bookshelf

The handsome and affecting volume representing three centuries of African American poetry leaps from the pages in this stirring audio rendition of the text, complete with biographical introductions of the poets and notes to aid the listening experience. This production represents twenty-five poets, including Phyllis Wheatley, W. E. B. DuBois, Paul Laurence Dunbar, Langston Hughes, Arna Bontemps, Countee Cullen, Maya Angelou, Rita Dove, Amiri Baraka, and others, offers much food for thought and discussion concerning slavery and the African American experience. Poetry is meant to be heard, and Bryan and Joshua-Porter do an excellent job conveying the intensity of the medium with their powerful performances. This is an excellent example of an audiobook enlarging the reading experience. A Common Core text exemplar for grades 6–8.

STANDARD—ENGLISH LANGUAGE ARTS

Students will be able to identify at least two ways in which poets use personification, figures of speech, and sound.

When it comes to learning how words sound and look and how meaning and emotion are communicated, nothing is better than sharing poetry out loud. Just try this: "Homework! Oh, homework! I hate you! You stink! I wish I could wash you away in the sink" by Jack Prelutsky and see and hear the irresistible pull of the words, the rhyme, the topic, and the emotional wallop. Kids *get* it. They hear it, they learn it, and very soon they can read it, too. Poetry is meant to be heard, to be spoken, to be shared. And poetry is available in more audio formats than ever before: podcasts on poet websites, audio archives of poetry readings on the Internet, YouTube recordings of kid poem performances, downloadable poetry audio files such as the Newbery Medal Book *Joyful Noise,* poetry anthologies packaged with CDs (such as *Poetry Speaks, Hip Hop Speaks to Children, My Hippo Has the Hiccups,* and *The Tree That Time Built,* all from Sourcebooks), and excellent audiobook adaptations of poetry books like the Odyssey Award–winning *Jazz* by Walter Dean Myers.

—Dr. Sylvia Vardell is a professor at the School of Library and Information Studies at Texas Women's University

---

Inkheart, written by Cornelia Funke, narrated by Lynn Redgrave, Listening Library

A mystery, a fantasy, and an excellent performance make *Inkheart* a wonderful listening experience. Twelve-year-old Meggy lives with her father, Mo, who is a magical bookbinder, one who can extract characters and things from a book and make them real. The introductory background music adds to the mysterious atmosphere as Meggy describes a house full of books, books everywhere that contain many characters, but stories that have exchanged her mother for the evil Capricorn. As Meggy discovers that she, too, has the magic, Capricorn appears to threaten her family again and the adventure begins.

STANDARD—ENGLISH LANGUAGE ARTS
Students will be able to understand and analyze complicated texts, including summary details and plot construction.

---

*Jazz,** written by Walter Dean Myers, illustrated by Christopher Myers, narrated by James "D-Train" Williams and Vaneese Thomas, Live Oak Media

This remarkable audiobook production takes three distinct media—poetry, painting, and music—and melds them into a unique and captivating whole. The original musical bed and the jazz readings of the two narrators broaden the effect of the poetry and the paintings by allowing listeners to absorb the words and the images as they are immersed in the music that is jazz. The individual tracks for each of the poems and the reading aloud of the glossary easily enable the listener to dip into the poetry or to revisit favorites. This feature of the production also increases its effectiveness for classroom use.

STANDARD—MUSIC
Students will compare the characteristic media of two or more arts to determine how similar events or ideas can be transformed into art.

Leviathan, written by Scott Westerfeld, narrated by Alan Cumming, Simon and Schuster Audio

In an alternate 1914, Europe is on the brink of war between the Darwinists (England and France), whose biotechnology has created living airships, and the Clankers (Germany and Austria), masters of mechanical engineering. Deryn Sharp has disguised herself as a boy to earn a spot as midshipman aboard the genetically engineered *Leviathan*, while Alek, son of the murdered Austrian archduke, flees his country in a mechanical walker. The meeting of the two teens in Switzerland sets the stage for this new series and provides many thoughtful and exciting moments. Cumming's interpretation complements Westerfeld's masterful world building, giving listeners the opportunity to take in both atmosphere and action. Cumming is especially adept at clarifying the growing relationship between Deryn and Alek, an important element of the story. The interview with Westerfeld at the end provides a fascinating explication of the steampunk genre and the variation on it that is presented in this book.

STANDARD—ENGLISH LANGUAGE ARTS

Students will compare and contrast fictional and historical accounts of the same period to understand how authors use or alter history.

Little Women, written by Louisa May Alcott, narrated by Lorelei King, BBC Audio

One of the best-loved classics of American children's literature, this chronicle of the March sisters and their struggle to survive emotionally and financially during the Civil War is on many reading lists and is a favorite for family listening. King's lively pacing keeps the story moving along, and her sympathetic vocal characterizations will charm listeners.

STANDARD—ENGLISH LANGUAGE ARTS

Students will read, understand, and discuss a wide range of complex texts, including drama, stories, and poems.

Lizzie Bright and the Buckminster Boy, written by Gary D. Schmidt, narrated by Sam Freed, Listening Library

The 2007 Newbery and Printz Honor story of Turner Buckminster and Lizzie Bright Griffin is based on true events. Turner arrives in Phippsburg, Maine, dreading the backwater life that his minister father has brought him to. That is, until he meets Lizzie, a free spirit who lives on nearby Malaga Island, which was founded by freed slaves. As Turner and Lizzie explore the Atlantic waters, the town leaders plot to move the islanders so that development can be planned. Freed's voice spins the tale with pacing that builds the narrative to its dramatic and tragic conclusion, one that changes Turner and Lizzie's lives forever.

STANDARD—HISTORY/SOCIAL STUDIES

Students will be able to recognize how the past helps us to understand the causes and results of events to analyze how beliefs from a historical period have unexpected consequences.

The Midnight Charter, written by David Whitley,
     narrated by Simon Vance, Macmillan
     Young Listeners

Mark and Lily, not far from their Title Days, when they must choose their life's work, live in the city state of Agora, where consumerism is rampant and everything—including life itself—can be bartered. As Mark becomes popular and wealthy as an astrologer, Lily sets a different course for her life, establishing an almshouse where she freely gives food and shelter. Their paths cross again as they become the principal figures in an ancient prophecy called the Midnight Charter. Vance's opulent voice and impeccable pacing provides the perfect entre into this dense, atmospheric, and thought-provoking story of a dystopian world.

STANDARD—ENGLISH LANGUAGE ARTS

Students will be able to read and interpret increasingly complex texts that present multiple points of view and sequence of events.

The Misfits, written by James Howe, narrated by
     Spencer Murphy and the Full Cast Family,
     Full Cast Audio

With a platform of "End name-calling once and for all!" four seventh graders form a third party to challenge the status quo during their school elections. Determined to take political action on their emotional dilemmas, Bobby ("Fatso"), Addie ("Beanpole" and "Know-It-All"), Skeezie ("Wop" and "Ree-tard"), and Joe ("Faggot") have been friends since elementary school precisely because, as Bobby says, "kids who get called the worst names oftentimes find each other." Written largely in dialogue, this coming-of-age story works particularly well in audio. Murphy, as Bobby, does a very effective job of representing the humor inherent in Bobby's character that allows him to navigate the difficulties of his young life. The other cast members also give spot-on performances, making listeners feel as if they were standing in the hallways of this small-town middle school.

STANDARD—HISTORY/SOCIAL STUDIES

Students will be able to identify and interpret varying forms of stereotyping, conformity, propaganda, and racism.

Mockingbird, written by Kathryn Erskine, narrated by Angela
   Jayne Rogers, Recorded Books

Ten-year-old Caitlin has Asperger's syndrome, which is making it even
more difficult to deal with the death of her beloved older brother, who
has been killed in a school shooting, and find closure for her father
and herself. Rogers's flat inflection and almost-stolid pacing brilliantly
characterize Caitlin's inner anguish, her inability to connect with
people, and her extreme lack of empathy. The emotional impact of this
2010 National Book Award for Young People winner is heightened by
Rogers's ability to draw listeners inside Caitlin's narrow world in a way
that words on a page alone cannot. Although Caitlin is in fifth grade,
the subject matter and the complexity of the situation make this a solid
choice for middle school students.

> STANDARD—ENGLISH LANGUA GE ARTS
> Students are able to distinguish between theme and topic in works
> of fiction.

The Mostly True Adventures of Homer P. Figg, written by
   Rodman Philbrick, narrated by William Dufris, Listening
   Library

Homer Figg spins a story cum tall tale set during the Civil War as he
journeys to find his brother, Harold, who has been sold into conscription.
Events of the Civil War, including some less well known, are embedded
into the story (e.g., hot-air balloon surveillance). Dufris's performance
is wonderful as he fully voices the gallery of memorable characters from
the varmints Stink and Smelt to Homer's quick, young colloquial twang.
The emotional range of the narration compels the listener to understand
Homer's horror at the Battle of Gettysburg and his gentle humor as
he continues his search. Also included are explanations of Civil War
definitions and slang.

> STANDARD—HISTORY/SOCIAL STUDIES
> Students will read and understand Civil War events and their impact on
> people's lives.

One Crazy Summer, written by Rita Williams-Garcia, narrated by
   SiSi Aisha Johnson, Recorded Books

Eleven-year-old Delphine and her two younger sisters are off to spend
the summer of 1968 in Oakland, California, with the mother who

abandoned them seven years earlier. Visions of beaches and Disneyland fill the heads of these girls from Brooklyn, New York, who have been raised by their father and grandmother. But when they arrive and meet their mother, reality is in harsh contrast to their vacation fantasies. Their mother does not want them and sends them off each day to a Black Panther community center where—for the first time—they confront African Americans who are actively struggling against racism and injustice. Johnson becomes Delphine, through whose eyes the story unfolds, with an unvoiced reading that describes the large cast of characters by subtle changes in inflection and pacing. By keeping her craft in the background, Johnson's narration shines the spotlight on Delphine's growing awareness of who she is and how she fits into her society. Winner of the 2010 Coretta Scott King Author Award and a 2010 Newbery Honor Book.

STANDARD—HISTORY/SOCIAL STUDIES
Students will examine examples of conflict and cooperation between and among cultural groups in society.

Peace, Locomotion, written by Jacqueline Woodson,
 narrated by Dion Graham, Brilliance Audio

Lonnie, a.k.a. "Locomotion," relates his story through letters to his nine-year-old sister, Lili. Living in separate foster families, Lonnie, now almost twelve, continues the story of *Locomotion,* and his writing still expresses his love and concern. He remembers about the "before" time when their parents were alive and hopes to share all his thoughts, poems, and dreams with Lili. Graham's resonant and soothing voice showcases the cadence of the narrative, bringing Lonnie's New York accent and lovely word imagery to the audio format. Lonnie's emotional turmoil and hopeful outlook are intertwined with everyday details of life in school and visits with Lili. This is a good choice for students who want to listen to an excellent example of writing and the use of language.

STANDARD—ENGLISH LANGUAGE ARTS
Students will be able to identify examples of figurative language, word imagery, and other literary devices.

The People Could Fly, written by Virginia Hamilton, narrated by
 Andrew Barnes, Audio Bookshelf

These remarkable retellings of twenty-four African American folktales by the late Virginia Hamilton beg to be read aloud, and Barnes does a superb job of bringing both intimacy and immediacy to this audio production. Following the organization of the print edition, the tales are divided into four CDs—tales of animals; the supernatural; the real, extravagant, and fanciful; and freedom tales—which makes it easy for teachers and families to choose favorite stories or those that are appropriate to specific classroom use. From the heartbreaking, yet hopeful titular story of those who flew away to escape the cruelty of slavery to the wonderful silliness of the well-known Tar Baby, listeners will revel in Hamilton's rich language, interpreted with humor and pathos by a skilled narrator. This is a Common Core text exemplar for grades 6–8.

STANDARD—ENGLISH LANGUAGE ARTS

Students will read, compare, and contrast a variety of literature, including short stories, novels, folktales, poetry, essays, and biographies.

Revenge of the Whale, written by Nathaniel Philbrick, narrated by Taylor Mali, Audio Bookshelf

On November 20, 1820, the whaleship *Essex* was rammed twice by an enormous sperm whale and sank two thousand nautical miles off the western coast of South America. Twenty-one sailors with little food and insufficient water set off in three small boats from the wreckage of the *Essex;* what followed was almost unbearably appalling. Using narratives left by two of the ship's survivors, Philbrick re-creates the harrowing tale of their struggle for survival. Mali's steady pacing and reportorial narrative style provide the appropriate distance from the horrific details of deprivation and cannibalism that plagued the unfortunate crew of the ship that is said to have provided Herman Melville with the idea for *Moby Dick.*

STANDARD—HISTORY/SOCIAL STUDIES

Students will discuss the influence of industrialization and its effect on the environment.

The Sea of Trolls, written by Nancy Farmer, narrated by Gerard Doyle, Recorded Books

In the year 793, a pillaging band of Norsemen snatch Jack and his little sister Lucy away from their Saxon coastal village. What ensues is a brilliant combination of history, horror, humor, and mythology. Jack's resulting quest is of epic proportions and leads naturally to discussions of friendship, community, and an individual's place in society. Doyle creates a unique voice for each character, real and imaginary, and keeps listeners enthralled to the end. Follow this up with its sequels: *The Land of the Silver Apples* and *The Islands of the Blessed*.

STANDARD—ENGLISH LANGUAGE ARTS
Students will recognize literary devises such as flashback, foreshadowing, and symbolism.

Seedfolks, written by Paul Fleischman, narrated by multiple
   voices, Audio Bookshelf

Picture an abandoned city lot—hard-packed dirt, broken glass, discarded tires—a mecca for vice and vermin. Now picture that same blighted landscape transformed into a thriving community garden through the efforts of thirteen neighborhood gardeners, young and old, from diverse backgrounds and distant lands. What is most amazing is that the metamorphosis does not stop with the garden but extends to the gardeners themselves, who gain strength from one another and become friends. A multiple cast of adult and child narrators give culturally authentic voice to Fleischman's powerful story, increasing the significance not only of the instructional value for civics classes but also of the emotional impact of this long-standing favorite of middle school students and teachers.

STANDARD—HISTORY/SOCIAL STUDIES
Students will describe how individuals and interest groups influence public policy decisions at the local level.

Skulduggery Pleasant, written by Derek Landy, narrated by
   Rupert Degas, HarperChildren's Audio

An over-the-top musical introduction, complete with screams, sets the stage for this sly and clever magical mystery. When twelve-year-old Stephanie Edgley inherits her late uncle's estate, she comes under the scrutiny of some very evil magical thugs and is rescued by a walking, talking skeleton! With great subtlety, Degas infuses every character with a unique voice, relishing the author's wit and sarcasm. The musical interludes between chapters add a wonderful extra element to a production that never disparages the intelligence of the audience.

STANDARD—ENGLISH LANGUAGE ARTS
Students will listen to, understand, and appreciate how literature can be enhanced by music, sound effects, and vocal performance.

The True Meaning of Smekday, written by Adam Rex, narrated by Bahni Turpin, Listening Library

A most improbable friendship, laugh-out-loud humor, and an exceptional performance combine to bring on-the-run Gratuity and J. Lo to a captivated listener. From invading aliens to a cross-country journey, Gratuity is writing her experiences for a time-capsule assignment, a story with layers of friendship; survival; and best of all, meeting life head-on with strong determination and fresh humor. The narration by Turpin showcases brilliant vocal characterizations and demonstrates the central factor that a fine audiobook production can serve to rise above the printed page. Any listener will find it difficult to forget the story—a worthy 2011 Odyssey Award winner.

STANDARD—ENGLISH LANGUAGE ARTS
Students will be able to compare and contrast a written and audio version of the same story and to analyze devices used in both.

Under the Blood Red Sun, written by Graham Salisbury, narrated by Jeff Woodman, Recorded Books

Thirteen-year-old Tomi Nakaji's life in pre–World War II Hawaii is largely uncomplicated. Sure, his family is poor—his fisherman father works hard—and his eccentric grandfather clings fiercely to their Japanese heritage, but Tomi's diverse group of friends gets along fine, united by a love of baseball. All of that changes on December 7, 1941, when Japan bombs Pearl Harbor. Suddenly, his father is suspected of aiding the enemy, his grandfather's Japanese flag is dangerous, and bigotry splinters his group of friends. Woodman's facility with culturally accurate accents enhances listeners' ability to enter Tomi's world by distinctly voicing Japanese, Portuguese, and native Hawaiian dialects in this excellent look at another aspect of America during the war.

STANDARD—HISTORY/SOCIAL STUDIES
Students will identify the causes and effects leading to American involvement in World War II, including the bombing of Pearl Harbor; students will be able to describe the impact of the war on the home front.

The Watsons Go to Birmingham—1963, written by Christopher
Paul Curtis, narrated by LeVar Burton, Listening Library

The year is 1963, and thirteen-year-old Byron Watson's pranks and
troublemaking have precipitated his family's summer trip from Flint,
Michigan, to Birmingham, Alabama. Little do they know that they are
traveling into one of history's black times, the day four young girls
were burned to death inside their church in Birmingham. LeVar Burton
distills Kenny's narrative voice with combined humor and distress as
the events unfold to describe that violent summer. The author has the
unusual ability to alternate comedy with drama as the Watsons encounter
vestiges of the segregated South interspersed with the hopes of the civil
rights movement. This 1996 Newbery Honor and Coretta Scott King
Author Honor title raises historical fiction to a high level.

> STANDARD—HISTORY/SOCIAL STUDIES
> Students will describe and understand events during the civil rights
> movement.

The Wednesday Wars, written by Gary D. Schmidt, narrated by
Joel Johnstone, Scholastic Audio

During the Vietnam War era, eighth grader Holling Hoodhood spends
Wednesday afternoons alone with a teacher he is sure hates him. All of his
classmates are off to religious education class, so Holling is relegated to
reading Shakespeare, a task he initially feels is a punishment. Instead, he
discovers friendship, how to stand up for himself, and—yes—gains an
appreciation of his reading assignments. Johnstone imbues this coming-
of-age story with an adolescent cadence that integrates well with the
narrative. What listener can resist touches of humor, awkward situations,
typical family life, and the foibles of school? This 2008 Newbery Honor
title could be used for many English language arts themes.

> STANDARD—ENGLISH LANGUAGE ARTS
> Students will be able to describe and analyze how characters, events,
> and plot develop over the course of a text.

When My Name Was Keoko, written by Linda Sue Park, narrated
by Jenny Ikeda and Norm Lee, Recorded Books

When the Japanese occupied Korea in 1910, they began a systematic
suppression of Korean culture, which culminated during World War II

with forcing the Korean population to give up not only their cultural identity but also their Korean names. Focusing on the years from 1940 to 1945, Park gives insight into how people lived under this harsh domination through the alternating voices of Sun-hee and her older brother Tae-yul, each choosing different methods of maintaining their traditions. Although Park employs subtle, yet clear distinctions between the two narrators, for inexperienced readers the two voices will be more easily delineated in the audio edition. Ikeda and Lee skillfully capture Sun-hee's scholarly, poetic nature and Tae-yul's angry defiance and provide accurate pronunciations of unfamiliar Korean and Japanese names and terms.

STANDARD—HISTORY/SOCIAL STUDIES
Students will demonstrate knowledge of the worldwide impact of World War II.

Woods Runner, written by Gary Paulsen, narrated by Danny Campbell, Listening Library

Set during the American Revolution, this is the story of Samuel, a woods runner, or wilderness expert. Returning home from hunting, he finds his home burned to the ground, his neighbors slaughtered, and his family missing. He uses his skills to track down his captured parents and plans their escape. The story is a realistic view of war and how Samuel copes with the horrible events. Campbell's voice successfully relates the story with vocal distinctions between characters that emphasize the setting and historical time. The story will especially attract boys who gravitate to war, gripping events, and engaging historical fiction.

STANDARD—ENGLISH LANGUAGE ARTS
Students will be able to compare a fictional account of a historical time with an information text of the same period, to understand how an author uses or alters the historical record.

7

Audiobooks and High School

Grades 9–12

*H*igh school students are poised on the threshold of a brave new world. They are mature one moment and childish the next. They have broad interests and reading habits, and they are busy all the time with school, sports, extracurricular activities, and jobs. Consummate multitaskers, they use audiobooks to "read" assignments while doing chores, working out, or riding the bus to sporting events. They squeeze in pleasure reading by listening while getting ready for school or while they're waiting to fall asleep at night. They are tech wizards who always have listening material on their mobile devices.

In this chapter you'll find an array of titles befitting the many moods and needs of high school students, whether to facilitate homework assignments or for that all-important reading for pleasure that enables teenagers to stay connected to the larger world.

The Absolutely True Story of a Part-Time Indian, written and
narrated by Sherman Alexie, Recorded Books

Sherman Alexie captures the sardonic persona and angst of the protagonist, Arnold Spirit, a.k.a. "Junior." In this contemporary story of Native American life on the Spokane reservation, teenager Junior faces the realities of family alcoholism, poverty, and overcoming disability to break stereotypes and obtain a good education. Alexie's cadence, tone, and inflection are true to the core of the story, as only the creator of the words can give. His voice is almost atonal, grasping Junior's humor and poetic language with small inflections and pacing. The performance surrounds the listener with the emotional swings of Junior's life but concludes with a hopeful outlook for this unique character. The story received both the 2007 National Book Award for Young People's Literature and the 2009 Odyssey Award for Excellence in Audiobook Production.

STANDARD—ENGLISH LANGUAGE ARTS
Students will be able to analyze an author's purpose in a story in which the style and narrative add to the power, persuasiveness, or beauty of the text.

Athletic Shorts, written by Chris Crutcher, narrated by Frank Muller, Recorded Books

Six short stories, most of which feature characters from Crutcher novels, center on boys, sports, love, parents, and life. Meet Angus Bethune, who is fat, has two sets of gay parents, and manages to have a glorious moment with the girl of his dreams. Or get to know Jack, who realizes that his father's racist views are all wrong when a black classmate rescues him from a gang attack. The struggles are palpable, not only because of Crutcher's gritty style and vivid writing but also because he brings to these narratives his background as an adolescent and family therapist. The late Frank Muller's steady, unvoiced delivery never calls attention to his narrative style, always placing the focus squarely on the individual stories and their characters.

STANDARD—ENGLISH LANGUAGE ARTS
Students will distinguish characteristics of various literary forms.

Bloody Jack: Being an Account of the Curious Adventures of Mary "Jacky" Faber, Ship's Boy, written by L. A. Meyer, narrated by Katherine Kellgren, Listen and Live Audio

Jacky Faber is happy as a ship's boy aboard the HMS *Dolphin*—no more scrounging and stealing just to get something to eat. The only problem is that Jacky's a girl, and she'll need plenty of courage and cleverness to keep up her disguise as she (and a rather motley crew) chases down dangerous pirates on the high seas. Kellgren becomes Jacky in this tour-de-force performance, capturing not only her Cheapside accent but also all of her spirit and pluck. Teens who get hooked by Jacky's adventures will be happy to listen to the many books that follow (seven and counting). Recipient of a 2008 Odyssey Honor.

> **STANDARD—ENGLISH LANGUAGE ARTS**
> Students will analyze how an author's choice of words influences the meaning and tone of a text, including a sense of time and place.

The Book Thief, written by Marcus Zusak, narrated by Allan Corduner, Listening Library

Death is the narrator of this exploration of the power of words to inspire, harm, and heal. The story is set in Nazi Germany during World War II, a time period that kept Death rather busy. When he sees young Leisel steal a book from her brother's gravesite, Death is intrigued and follows the girl and her relationships with her foster family and community through years of stealing books. Death calls this a "small story," but of course it is not, as it touches on all that is best and worst in human interactions. Corduner's detached reading mines the depths of Death's observations, often laden with irony, yet laced with humor. Conversely, Corduner brings unique voicing to Leisel, her family, and her community. This 2007 Michael L. Printz Honor Book is also a Common Core text exemplar for grades 9–10.

> **STANDARD—ENGLISH LANGUAGE ARTS**
> Students will determine a theme or central idea in a text and examine its development over the course of the text.

The Boy Who Dared, written by Susan Campbell Bartoletti, narrated by David Ackroyd, Listening Library

In this fictionalized biography, we find a portrait of Helmuth Hübener, a German teenager executed for his resistance to the Nazis. On the basis of research and original sources, Susan Campbell Bartoletti crafts a compelling and gripping novel about a German teen dedicated to sharing the truth about Hitler's war. Helmuth stood up to the Nazis and paid with his life. Written in present-tense flashbacks, the tale traces Helmuth's early life in Hamburg, his gradual and heroic resistance to Hitler, and his final days imprisoned for distributing anti-Nazi leaflets. This powerful story is narrated with consistent voicing and German inflections and includes some sound effects that add to the tension. An ideal pairing with *Hitler Youth: Growing Up in Hitler's Shadow* by the same author.

STANDARD—HISTORY/SOCIAL STUDIES
Students will describe and understand events surrounding resistance
within Germany to Hitler's Nazi Germany.

Buddha Boy, written by Kathe Koja, narrated by
    Spencer Murphy and the Full Cast Family,
    Full Cast Audio

Justin worries that he will be unable to maintain his invisibility when
he's paired with the new, weird kid Jinsen—known as Buddha Boy to
the bullies—for a school project. Sharing a love of art, Justin and Jinsen
slowly become friends, and Justin learns that it's important to honor your
own sense of self. Koja's disjointed writing style works well with this
full-cast recording, allowing the voices of the various narrators to expand
on Justin's path to self-awareness. Murphy ably conveys Justin's fear of
the unknown, and the author's note read by Koja will prompt discussion
of the writing process as well as conversations about dealing with bullies.

STANDARD—HEALTH
Students will learn strategies to reduce and prevent violence and
implement peaceful resolution of conflicts.

Bury My Heart at Wounded Knee: An Indian History
    of the American West, written by Dee Brown,
    narrated by Grover Gardner, Blackstone Audio

Brown's account of the systematic removal and near annihilation of
American Indians from 1860 to 1890 marks the beginning of an American
examination of an expanded, less Eurocentric view of our history. Although
there are those who argue that Brown glosses over the less savory aspects
of Native American culture, there is no disputing the importance of his
book to the study of westward expansion. Gardner proves himself more
than able to navigate the stormy waters of the text, bringing to it a smooth
interpretation that is neither dispassionate nor over the top. His facility
with pronouncing the many American Indian names will aid students in
their study of this Common Core Standards text exemplar for grades 9–10.

STANDARD—HISTORY/SOCIAL STUDIES
Students will examine and explain different points of view of the same
historical event.

The Call of the Wild, written by Jack London, narrated by Jeff
   Daniels, Listening Library

Students will be newly introduced to a classic story, a story that was
first published in 1903 and has maintained its authentic narrative. The
journey of an Alaskan sled dog, Buck, is as fresh today as it was more
than one hundred years ago. Daniels grippingly narrates this poignant
Arctic survival story with excellent pacing and vocal resonance. Buck
learns harsh lessons from the humans who use him, and his instinct is
finally resolved when he watches and interacts with a pack of wolves.
The urge for freedom slowly but surely engulfs him, and the listener
cannot but cheer and applaud his courage and strength. This is an
audiobook experience that students will certainly enjoy.

STANDARD—ENGLISH LANGUAGE ARTS
Students will be able to recognize and analyze how an author's choice
of language, plot, and events in a story result in literary effects such as
tension or surprise.

Carter Finally Gets It, written by Brent Crawford, narrated by
   Nick Podehl, Brilliance Audio

Fourteen-year-old Carter is starting high school and finding adolescent
crises at every turn in this humorous and realistic take on teen relationships. Contrasting Carter's everyday angst with comedic situations, Nick
Podehl is spot on in his vocal characterization. His energetic portrayal
of Carter, his friends, and the adults they encounter captures the daily
turmoil of high school life. The narrative is definitely for older teens,
with descriptions and vernacular that could offend some, but the down-
to-earth portrayal of the high school academic and social scene is both
engaging and informative.

STANDARD—HISTORY/SOCIAL STUDIES
Students will recognize that their personal identity is influenced by their
culture, group, and institutions, and that shared experiences affect their
individual development.

Chapters from My Autobiography, written by Mark Twain,
   narrated by Bronson Pinchot, BBC Audiobooks America

Nearing the end of his life, Twain determined to recount his life for
posterity. Naturally, being Twain he did it in his own inimitable fashion

talking "about the matter which for the moment its interest for me is exhausted." This makes for a meandering, complex structure "whereby the past and the present are constantly brought face to face." Pinchot's lazy drawl effectively highlights the humor, and his conversational tone is wholly appropriate to the text, whereas his sometimes punchy pacing directs the listener's attention to important details. Students will get an understanding of the life experiences that shaped Twain's writing and will feel as if Twain himself were in the room talking to them. A reading of "The Celebrated Jumping Frog of Calaveras County" concludes this fine production.

STANDARD—ENGLISH LANGUAGE ARTS
Students will read, interpret, and discuss a wide range of literature to understand themselves, the culture of the United States, and the world.

The Circuit: Stories from the Life of a Migrant Child,
written by Francisco Jiménez, narrated by Adrian Vargas,
Audio Bookshelf

In a series of related short stories, Jiménez tells the story of Panchito's life as a migrant worker from the time he leaves Mexico with his family for a better life in the United States through his high school graduation. Years of backbreaking work, poverty, and moving from place to place are described with honesty; there is no romanticizing of this story, yet the love and strength of this family's story remains intact. Vargas skillfully translates Panchito's tale at every age, and the Spanish names and words flow easily. Several musical interludes are included, and the interview with Jiménez at the end has additional instructional use.

STANDARD—ENGLISH LANGUAGE ARTS
Students will examine the characteristics of a variety of literary formats; students will describe the use of images and sounds to elicit readers' emotions.

Dairy Queen, written by Catherine Gilbert Murdock, narrated by
Natalie Moore, Listening Library

D. J. Schwenk's life on her family's Wisconsin dairy farm mirrors the adolescent work-in-progress scenario. At fifteen, she dutifully works to complete the daily chores of the Schwenk Farm, a farm where the cows are named after football players. This alone gives a glimpse of the wry humor that is enhanced by Moore's authentically midwestern, adolescent sardonic tone, adding to D. J.'s very appealing character. When her father's injury leaves a major void in the farm routine, star quarterback Brian works in exchange for D. J.'s training help. Complications ensue as D. J. competes for a spot on her school's football team and her secret crush on Brian grows. Moore's partial voicing individualizes D. J.'s family and friends and bring out the humor of this engaging story. All this and football, too, will attract teen listeners, who will want to listen to the follow-ups of this first novel, *The Off Season* and *Front and Center* (also narrated by Moore).

STANDARD—ENGLISH LANGUAGE ARTS

Students will be able to analyze how characters develop and interact with other characters to advance the plot or theme.

David Copperfield, written by Charles Dickens, narrated by Simon Vance, Tantor Media

Dickens's famous bildungsroman follows sensitive young David from birth to his eventual maturity as a successful writer and husband. In between, there is a great deal of Victorian drama—a wicked stepfather, an evil headmaster, a lovely but vapid young woman, and more. On many high school and college reading lists, *David Copperfield* is a bit difficult to stick with because of its length and complexity. Enter Vance, with his superlative pacing and his ability to precisely phrase Dickens's dense text. His voicing of the many odd characters that populate the tale will delight teen listeners. At thirty-four hours, this is a very long audiobook, but Vance pulls out all the stops, reveling in the humor and melodrama of the story.

STANDARD—ENGLISH LANGUAGE ART

Students will be able to examine a literary selection from several critical perspectives and explain the influence of historical context on the form, style, and point of view of the text.

Does My Head Look Big in This? written by Randa Abdel-Fattah, narrated by Rebecca Macaulay, Bolinda Audio

All teens ask the same essential question: "How do I fit into my world?" But the answers for one Muslim teenager may be quite different from the average American student experience. Amal has always seemed like an ordinary Australian teen of Palestinian decent until the day she decides to wear the hijab, the traditional head covering for Muslim women, full-time. This decision pits her against school administration and forces a reexamination of relationships with everyone—from family to friends, neighbors, and even the non-Muslim Adam, on whom she has a crush. Macaulay's rapid-fire narration sounds authentically teen and allows American listeners to get a better feel for the Australian slang that peppers the text.

STANDARD—ENGLISH LANGUAGE ARTS
Students will explore a point of view or cultural experience in works of literature outside the United States.

Ernest Hemingway: A Writer's Life, written by Catherine Reef, narrated by Jill Shellabarger, Oasis Audio

A well-written biography of the larger-than-life twentieth-century author that includes many interesting facts and is told in good narrative form. Hemingway's unconventional life, from his time in various parts of the world (Paris, Florida Keys, Toronto, Cuba, and Idaho) to his marriages, children, bullfighting, fishing, hunting, and his World War I and II experiences, are all told in an engaging format. Above all, however, is his writing, and background information about *The Sun Also Rises*, *A Farewell to Arms*, *Death in the Afternoon*, *For Whom the Bell Tolls*, and *The Old Man and the Sea* fills in details for the listener. From the musical introduction to the narrator's matter-of-fact, crisp voice, this biographical narrative translates well to audio and should encourage listeners to search for, read, or listen to Hemingway. This title would be a fine pairing with *The Old Man and the Sea*.

STANDARD—ENGLISH LANGUAGE ARTS
Students will be able to analyze how an author uses source materials to present information for a specific topic.

Feed, written by M. T. Anderson, narrated by David Aaron Baker, Listening Library

Imagine a not-so-distant future in which your laptop and your smartphone are connected in your head. Your brain includes dictionaries and encyclopedias, and you can talk to your friends whenever you like. Sound good? Now imagine pop-up advertising in your brain. Envision a society where language is becoming a forgotten art, where consumerism is rampant, and where everything is dying. This is the world of the feed, where many indulge in mind-altering experiences to combat boredom. Baker's unvoiced reading, relying on pitch-perfect inflection and flawless timing, ably portrays the tedium as well as the disintegration of language that leaves both teens and adults—including the president of the United States—substituting vulgar terms for proper words they can no longer remember. Anderson does not glorify any of this, but uses it to support his thesis of a world going bad—one not too dissimilar from our own. Anderson's dystopia is made chillingly real in this production by the inclusion of a full cast portraying the feed.

STANDARD—ENGLISH LANGUAGE ARTS
Students will analyze how an author's choice of structure contributes to the meaning of the text.

The Fellowship of the Ring, written by J. R. R. Tolkien, narrated by Rob Inglis, Recorded Books

The first book in Tolkien's epic Lord of the Rings trilogy sees the formation of the fellowship that must destroy the mystical ring created by the Dark Lord Sauron on Mount Doom. Tolkien created a host of fantastic characters to people his world—hobbits, elves, dwarves, and more—to tell this classic tale of the battle between good and evil. In this fine production, Inglis intensifies the folkloric quality of the text with distinctive voices that distinguish between the upright and the malevolent. His command of Tolkien's invented Elvish language is remarkable and removes from listeners the necessity to determine pronunciation. For those students who have difficulty with Tolkien's dense text, Inglis provides a stellar entrée into these exciting stories as he also narrates *The Two Towers* and *The Return of the King*.

STANDARD—ENGLISH LANGUAGE ARTS
Students will recognize archetypes, motifs, and symbols in literary texts.

The Great Gatsby, written by F. Scott Fitzgerald, narrated by Frank Muller, Recorded Books

Fitzgerald's complex, tightly plotted novel of modern (1920s) life is rendered comprehensible for high school students through Muller's faultless phrasing. He effortlessly delineates the linguistic disparities between classes and regions in this false society, highlighting the deceit underlying Gatsby's self-invention. The rhythms of the text and the richness of the language come to the fore when listening to Muller's opulent voice. This is a Common Core College and Career Readiness (CCR) text exemplar for grade 11.

STANDARD—ENGLISH LANGUAGE ARTS

Students will read, understand, and be able to discuss a variety of texts representing American literature, history, and culture.

Hamlet, written by William Shakespeare, narrated by Simon
Russell Beale, Imogen Stubbs, Jane Lapotaire, and a full cast,
BBC Audiobooks America

Shakespeare's longest play, *Hamlet* is also one of his most famous. In this tragedy, the young prince exacts revenge on his uncle for the murder of his father, the king. The scope of Shakespearean language and poetry is best understood when read aloud, and this production, with its more-than-competent cast, eases the path for the average high school student who struggles to discover the meaning buried in the text. Musical interludes and an insert detailing the tracks with a scene-by-scene summary increase the utility for student use. A Common Core CCR text exemplar for grade 11.

STANDARD—ENGLISH LANGUAGE ARTS

Students will compare and contrast ways in which character and dialogue advance theme and dramatic effect.

The writings of Shakespeare are another great triumph of audiobooks. How many student readers have had their interest in Shakespeare killed by the act of just reading Shakespeare? These are stories that were written to be spoken, moaned, yelled, performed.

—Jon Scieszka, children's book author and 2008 Library of Congress
Ambassador for Young People's Literature

Here in Harlem: Poems in Many Voices, written by Walter Dean
Myers, narrated by multiple voices, Live Oak Media

This lively, authentic, and poetic tribute to the lives and people of Harlem is presented with music and background sound effects that lift the narrative to an exceptional high. A stellar ensemble cast and an introduction read by the author give the listener a memorable collection of characters, from Delia Pierce, age thirty-two, hairdresser, to Homer Grimes, age eighty-three, blind war veteran. Interspersed with jazz and street sounds, this wonderful production can be purchased as a read-along (with period photographs, graphics, and a map of Harlem) but can also stand on its own. This audiobook can improve any poetry unit.

STANDARD—ENGLISH LANGUAGE ARTS
Students will be able to interpret and analyze poetry, including meaning and aesthetic impact.

Hitler Youth: Growing Up in Hitler's Shadow, written by
  Susan Campbell Bartoletti, narrated by Kathrin Kana,
  Listening Library

Innovation and creativity in information audiobooks are demonstrated in this Newbery Honor Book with facts and information that gradually leave the listener to become aware of the implications of Hitler's plans for Germany and the Hitler Youth. The exploitation of Germany's young bought their devotion to the Nazi cause while blinding them to the true motives behind Hitler's quest for power. As World War II comes to a close, the role of the Hitler Youth, from manning flak guns and searchlights to fighting fires from bomb raids indicates how they contributed to the war effort. Kana's steady voice propels the narrative forward to its conclusion without diminishing the brutality. A critical and effective supplement is a captioned photograph slide-show that provides a dramatic culmination to the narrative. As an example, the listener hears the story of Hans and Sophie Scholl, who became disaffected from the Hitler Youth and formed the White Rose Resistance group. Knowing their story and fate, it becomes even more powerful to see their faces in the slideshow. An added bonus is an introduction and epilogue spoken by the author. An ideal pairing with *The Boy Who Dared.*

STANDARD—HISTORY/SOCIAL STUDIES
Students will be able to analyze historical events in primary and secondary sources to determine how key events developed; students will be able to understand and analyze events surrounding Nazi Germany's use of power during World War II.

I Know Why the Caged Bird Sings, written and narrated by Maya
    Angelou, Books on Tape

Finally, there is an unabridged edition of poet Angelou's autobiographical work. Eloquently read by the author, the story of her hardscrabble life growing up with a variety of family members in the Deep South, in St. Louis, and in Southern California. Her rise above racism, rape, and teenage pregnancy is remarkable, and no one could tell this story out loud as well as the author herself. This Common Core text exemplar for grades 9–10 is on many high school reading lists but will also make for an involving family listen.

STANDARD—ENGLISH LANGUAGE ARTS

Students will read and analyze a variety of informational texts, including biographies and autobiographies.

Jerk, California, written by Jonathan Friesen, narrated by Andy
    Paris, Recorded Books

High school senior Sam has lived with Tourette's syndrome since he was six years old. His abusive stepfather has cemented Sam's self-loathing; he has no friends and no prospects for college or work after graduation. Hired by George, the town eccentric, Sam begins to learn that the father from whom he inherited Tourette's was an entirely different person from what he's been led to believe. When George dies unexpectedly, Sam sets off on a quest to discover the truth about his father and himself. The intrusion of Sam's inner dialogue mirrors his jerky muscles, and Paris reads with matter-of-fact voicing and steady pacing, keeping the listener firmly anchored to the action. Winner of the 2009 Schneider Family Book Award.

STANDARD—ENGLISH LANGUAGE ARTS

Students will be able to make predictions, interpret inferences, and link prior knowledge to increase their reading comprehension.

The Killer's Cousin, written by Nancy Werlin, narrated by Nick
    Podehl, Brilliance Audio

David Jaffe, living with the guilt of accidentally killing his girlfriend, has moved from Baltimore to Cambridge, Massachusetts, to complete his senior year of high school while living with his aunt and uncle and his eleven-year-old cousin, Lily, herself a very disturbed child. In attempting to uncover the meaning behind strange and increasingly alarming incidents, David exposes Lily's terrible secret. Podehl's narration sounds realistically adolescent and is expertly paced to heighten the tension built by Werlin's text. The eerie music that begins and ends each disc adds to the mystery of this teen thriller.

STANDARD—ENGLISH LANGUAGE ARTS

Students will interpret and analyze how an author creates a story structure using suspense and tension that affect the narrative impact.

King of the Mild Frontier: An Ill-Advised Autobiography, written and narrated by Chris Crutcher, Listening Library

Crutcher, who is almost single-handedly responsible for pushing the envelope of acceptable themes and language in young adult literature, narrates his own story with great good humor. He doesn't shy away from the low points of his life, but he always makes the connections that help teens understand how to get back on the right track. Sometimes it's luck, but mostly it's hard work, and Crutcher relates that, too. Biography, because of its narrative structure, is a natural for audio, and listening to the man who lived through all of this drama makes *King of the Mild Frontier* even better. Pair this with any of Crutcher's fiction for a fascinating author study.

STANDARD—ENGLISH LANGUAGE ARTS

Students will read and analyze a variety of informational materials, including biographies and autobiographies.

The Namesake, written by Jhumpa Lahiri, narrated by Sarita Choudhoury, Books on Tape

Forty years of the lives of the Ganguli family begin with the arranged marriage of Americanized Ashoke and his traditional Bengali wife, Ashima. How they and the succeeding generations adjust to life in the United States or cling fiercely to Bengali ways makes for a fascinating glimpse into an immigrant experience. Choudhoury is well able to authentically voice both American and Bengali accents and her smooth narration places the focus on the search for fulfillment and social acceptance that is at the heart of this novel. A Common Core CCR text exemplar for grade 11.

STANDARD—ENGLISH LANGUAGE ARTS

Students will examine points of view or cultural experiences revealed in literary texts.

Newes from the Dead, written by Mary Hooper, narrated by
    Rosalyn Landor and Michael Page, Brilliance Audio

Based on factual events in history and set in 1650, Anne Greene is wrongfully tried for murdering her newborn son. The gruesome introduction, in which Anne is literally waking from the dead, alternates between the voices of Anne and Robert, an Oxford scholar witnessing her revival. Landor and Page marvelously perform the tale of cruelty, culture, and social class separation. Their slight British accents are well paced and distinct, and bring clarity of emotion to the strong narrative pull. Descriptions of medieval manor and village life are heightened by background sound effects (e.g., the raucous crowd at the hanging). A strong addition is the reading of the actual pamphlet that was written and published at the time, *Newes from the Dead*.

STANDARD—ENGLISH LANGUAGE ARTS
Students will be able to understand and identify devices used in historical fiction and recognize fact from fiction.

Norman Tuttle on the Last Frontier, written and narrated by Tom
    Bodett, Listening Library

Fifteen intertwined stories follow an Alaskan teen from thirteen-year-old awkwardness to sixteen-year-old self-assurance. Norman's struggles with his first job, first love, and first deer hunt are lessons in what not to do and will be recognizable to teenagers everywhere. Bodett's humorous and casual style is perfect as the voice of this appealing young man. He not only imbues Norman and his father with great personality but also manages to make the geography as lifelike as the human characters to whom he gives voice.

STANDARD—ENGLISH LANGUAGE ARTS
Students will be able to read and discuss literary texts that represent a particular point of view and/or cultural experience.

The Old Man and the Sea, written by Ernest Hemingway, narrated
    by Donald Sutherland, Simon and Schuster Audio

A fish tale, a survival story, a moral challenge—all that and Hemingway's lyrical prose are brought to the listener by the impeccable voicing of Sutherland. With exquisite pacing and inflection, Sutherland expands the story of Santiago, an old Cuban fisherman engaging in a literal and figurative battle with a huge marlin. Filled with ironic twists, lovely visual imagery, and poignant moments, this classic has survived the test of time. This title can be paired with *Ernest Hemingway: A Writer's Life.*

STANDARD—ENGLISH LANGUAGE ARTS

Students will recognize narrative techniques such as pacing, description, reflection, and plot lines that develop characters and events.

Pride and Prejudice, written by Jane Austen, narrated by Emilia Fox, Naxos AudioBooks

Unmarried daughters from a family in somewhat straightened circumstances; single young men "in possession of a good fortune"; a silly, gossipy mother and a detached father—add in a deliciously sparkling reading by Fox and Austen's most famous novel springs to life. Fox's light voice resonates with all the solemnity and outrageousness of Regency society, infusing each character with distinct personality. Be sure to give this to students who struggle to understand Austen's humor. A Common Core CCR text exemplar for grade 11.

STANDARD—ENGLISH LANGUAGE ARTS

Students will be able to recognize and explain how an author's choice of setting, plot, characters, and other story elements affect the impact and meaning of the narrative.

Private Peaceful, written by Michael Morpurgo, narrated by Jeff Woodman, Recorded Books

A series of flashbacks relates the story of inseparable teenaged brothers whose lives and loves are irrevocably changed by World War I. Lying about his age, Thomas "Tommo" Peaceful enlists to follow his brother Charlie, a decision that brings brutal trench warfare, gas attacks, and death. Told in a first-person narrative and flawlessly rendered by a fully voiced reading, this candidly demonstrates to students the horrors of war. The performance showcases a story that is made even more powerful with the listening.

STANDARD—HISTORY/SOCIAL STUDIES

Students will be able to analyze and report historical events to determine cause-and–effect relationships.

***The Ruby in the Smoke* (Sally Lockhart Mysteries),** written by
Philip Pullman, narrated by Anton Lesser, Listening Library

The scene is Victorian London, where sixteen-year-old Sally Lockhart
is grieving for her murdered father. With hair-raising speed, Sally is
engulfed in a thrilling mystery, one in which Lesser's British accent
highlights the wonderful use of language. Even the dramatization of a
character's sudden collapse is done with theatrical flair, as Sally begins
unraveling the mystery surrounding her father's death. The narration is
fully voiced and heightened by the well-done interactive conversations.
From the simple words "seven blessings" to the titular ruby, the plot
brings Sally into danger as secrets chase and threaten her—secrets that
are solved in a satisfying conclusion. This is the first title in a trilogy that
includes *The Shadow in the North* and *The Tiger in the Well*.

STANDARD—ENGLISH LANGUAGE ARTS
Students will be able to understand how language is used in different
contexts to fully comprehend when reading or listening.

***Sabriel* (The Abhorsen Trilogy, Book 1),** written by Garth Nix,
narrated by Tim Curry, Listening Library

Nix's eloquence with words is on full display with the incomparable
Curry as narrator. His low baritone introduces this fully voiced performance featuring Sabriel, an eighteen-year-old necromancer. The
high drama of this finely wrought fantasy brings an unusual twist to
the familiar good-versus-evil theme as Sabriel begins her journey to
free her father, the Abhorsen, who is trapped in Death. She encounters
obstacles and strange creatures while she attempts to free the dead to
their rest and accept her destiny as her father's heir. Listeners will be
happy to continue the story with *Lirael* and *Abhorsen*, with Curry again
as narrator.

STANDARD—ENGLISH LANGUAGE ARTS
Students will summarize, discuss, and analyze complicated plot structures, including development of characters, themes, and conclusions.

Saint Joan, written by Bernard Shaw, narrated by Amy Irving, Edward
Herrmann, Kristoffer Tabori, and a full cast, Blackstone Audio

Shaw's dramatic recreation of Joan of Arc—who she really was and
how she affected the times in which she lived—works particularly well

as an audio presentation because the action is so visual. Largely didactic in purpose, the play is also filled with romance, tragedy, and farce. The acting is superb and the voices of this impressive cast blend nicely with one another. Hearing this read aloud enhances the humor and tension inherent in the text.

STANDARD—ENGLISH LANGUAGE ARTS

Students will be able to interpret and analyze a narrative or drama from different eras and cultures.

A Savage Thunder, written by Jim Murphy, narrated by Kevin Orton, Recorded Books

Good nonfiction can be disguised as a story, and this one chronicles the Civil War battle that was devastating and critical to both sides. Extensive use of quotes, letters, songs, and poems are narrated by Orton's reporterlike voice, which adds to the informational tone. The political, economic, tactical, and human toll of the war is established through the historical importance of the Battle of Antietam. Even small details such as the presence of Clara Barton add to the impact of the narrative. While listening, students could increase their understanding if some battle maps are available.

STANDARD—HISTORY/SOCIAL STUDIES

Students will be able to describe significant events of the Civil War, especially the critical Battle of Antietam.

Saving Francesca, written by Melina Marchetta, narrated by Rebecca Macauley, Bolinda Audio

Being one of the first female students in the newly co-ed St. Sebastian's School is difficult enough for high school student Francesca, but when her strong mother suddenly spirals into depression, life seems to be taking a downward turn. By turns funny and poignant, the novel is brilliantly conveyed through Macaulay's spot-on narration. Whether she's reading teen escapades at breakneck speed or pausing to let listeners digest Francesca's emotional turmoil, Macaulay is the perfect interpreter for this engaging Australian import.

STANDARD—ENGLISH LANGUAGE ARTS

Students will be able to explain how an author's plot structure, word choices, tone, and voice affect the meaning and purpose of the narrative.

Sleeping Freshmen Never Lie, written by David Lubar, narrated
by Ryan MacConnell and the Full Cast Family, Full Cast Audio

Scott Hudson is not sure what to expect from his freshman year in high school, but it certainly doesn't include his mother being pregnant! When he becomes the target of the school bully, friends desert him, and his older brother gets arrested, he resorts to the journal he is writing (boys don't write diaries, so it is definitely *not* a diary!) to his unborn sibling, offering advice on how to survive high school. Scott makes full use of the writing styles he learns about in his English class, writing a sports report as a series of Tom Swifties and employing stream of consciousness in his journal entries to the "fluid-dwelling piece of protoplasm." MacConnell gives a spot-on performance as the hapless Scott, and the production works particularly well in creating his thoughts—separated from the rest of the story by musical interludes—as he writes in his journal. No one will fall asleep listening to this one.

STANDARD—ENGLISH LANGUAGE ARTS
Students will use literary terms to describe text selections.

A Step from Heaven, written by An Na, narrated by Jina Oh,
Listening Library

As Young Ju learns to speak English, assimilates into a new culture, and gains confidence, her parents are forced to alter their traditional Korean way of life to that of American society. Family pressures and emotional turmoil threaten Young Ju's outlook as she grows to assert her independence. Oh's sensitive narration highlights the struggle of the immigrant family in this 2002 Michael L. Printz Award winner, a story whose strong plot will grab the listener until the final chapter.

STANDARD—ENGLISH LANGUAGE ARTS
Students will be able to identify themes and how they are resolved
in a novel, including a description and summary of plot, setting, and
character development.

The Three Documents That Made America: The Declaration of Independence, the Constitution of the U.S.A., and the Bill of Rights, narrated by Terry Bregy, with introductions written and read by Sam Fink, Audio Bookshelf

At some point in their high school curriculum, every American student must study these documents, and many find them rather dry and difficult reading. This audiobook comes to the rescue. Fascinating introductions give brief but critical prefatory information, and Bregy's measured, firm tones underscore the beauty of the prose and the courage of those who drafted these iconic words. The Declaration of Independence and the Bill of Rights are Common Core CCR text exemplar for grade 11.

STANDARD—HISTORY/SOCIAL STUDIES
Students will understand the political ideas that shaped revolutionary America and led to the creation of the Declaration of Independence; students will understand the difficulties of forming the new nation and the historical development of the Constitution.

To Kill a Mockingbird, written by Harper Lee, narrated by Sissy
    Spacek, Harper Audio

What do you do when everything you know and believe as a young girl is turned upside down? This is the dilemma facing Scout when her father, a lawyer, takes on the defense of a black man accused of raping a white girl. Spacek's lilting Southern accent provides the perfect medium for Harper Lee's Pulitzer Prize–winning classic story of a small Southern town's descent into racial bigotry. Told by child narrator Scout Finch, this staple of high school reading lists is made even more powerful and poignant through this unvoiced, measured performance. A Common Core text exemplar for grades 9–10.

STANDARD—ENGLISH LANGUAGE ARTS
Students will read and study classic and contemporary American literature, identifying themes and characterizations that reflect history and culture.

Treasure Island, written by Robert Louis Stevenson, narrated by
    Alfred Molina, Listening Library

The swashbuckling classic involving a young boy, Jim Hawkins; a foolish squire; an adventuresome doctor; and a menacing pirate in search of buried treasure is often a difficult read for high school students unfamiliar with the highly descriptive writing style of the past. This production comes to their rescue, with fluid, evocative narration by Molina, who manages to capture each character in this vast story. His rich, deep voice crackles with menace as Long John Silver while maintaining just the right timbre for young Jim. The opening music that follows the introduction sets the tone, and the singing of sea shanties enhances the period authenticity. The afterword by maritime scholar David Cordingly makes this especially useful for high school classrooms.

STANDARD—ENGLISH LANGUAGE ARTS
Students will read British literature and relate the works to themes and issues of their eras.

A Tree Grows in Brooklyn, written by Betty Smith, narrated by
  Kate Burton, Caedmon Audio

In this classic story, the listener enters a time capsule and becomes a witness to early-twentieth-century tenement life in the Williamsburg neighborhood of Brooklyn, New York. Francie Nolan introduces her family, a family coping with poverty but hoping for a better future. Burton's wonderful narration enhances a "you are there" atmosphere, and her voice variations bring the neighborhood to life. The story follows Francie, only a child at the opening, to when she is grown and following her dreams. This audiobook will introduce a novel that has been enjoyed by several generations and will demonstrate why the story has endured.

STANDARD—ENGLISH LANGUAGE ARTS
Students will be able to understand and describe how the use of language and style affects the meaning of a story and the resulting implication to reading or listening comprehension.

Troy, written by Adèle Geras, narrated by Miriam Margolyes,
  Listening Library

The last days of Troy are seen through the eyes of young people who have been permanently altered by the long, brutal war. The capriciousness and cruelty of the gods play out in the intrigue and drama unfolding in the lives of those remaining in Troy. The fully voiced, tour-de-force reading is extremely well done by Margolyes, especially the voices of three serving women who act as the Greek chorus. The story will help students understand Greek history and the structure of Greek drama.

STANDARD—ENGLISH LANGUAGE ARTS
Students will be able to identify the characteristics that distinguish literary forms and explain the influence of historical context on the form, style, and point of view of a written work.

The Whale Rider, written by Witi Ihimaera, narrated by Jay
    Laga'aia, Bolinda Audiobooks

The book that inspired the award-winning film opens with the Maori
legend of the original whale rider, introducing American teens to a
culture they may not know. When the birth of a girl child—Kahu—
breaks the chain of male descendants, her paternal grandfather rejects
her, throwing the family and the community into disarray. Jay Laga'aia,
as Uncle Rawiri, tells Kahu's story, effortlessly navigating the Maori
names and New Zealand slang, allowing listeners to concentrate on
the story's characters and their move from traditional beliefs to a new
cultural awareness.

STANDARD—ENGLISH LANGUAGE ARTS
Students will investigate points of view and cultural experiences in
literature from outside the United States.

Your Own, Sylvia, written by Stephanie Hemphill, narrated by a
    full cast, Listening Library

This creative, personal, and intense fictionalized biography of Sylvia
Plath is told in verse. The cadence and format of the performance
combines with clarity and affection to present the volatile life of Plath.
Her friends and family make an interesting range of characters and
perspectives, and the narrative is interspersed with footnotes by the
author. The voices of Aurelia Plath and Ted Hughes are especially fine
as they contribute their thoughts to create a broad view of Plath's life.
This title would make a good companion for students who have been
assigned *The Bell Jar* and want to know more about the complex life of
this poet-author.

STANDARD—ENGLISH LANGUAGE ARTS
Students will be able to analyze how an author chooses to structure a
story that contributes to its meaning and aesthetic impact.

8
~
Connecting It All

Audiobooks, Literacy, and Instructional Themes

One of the most creative parts of working with young people, whether in a classroom, a library, or at home, is developing what to teach or learn, when, and with what materials. This is true of our work with audiobooks and literacy, finding the just-right audiobook for the just-right listener at the just-right time. It may appear obvious, but all well-designed lessons tie resources to learning objectives, so selecting titles according to grade level and subject are key ingredients to integrating audiobooks into core curriculum. For us, this is the fun part, putting it all together, developing ideas for how to use audiobooks, especially with young people in educational settings. Audiobook titles, learning standards, and curricular themes can be put together with strategies to use in various settings. All the following suggestions demonstrate how excellent audiobooks support literacy skills, and all the examples listed use specific titles that have been annotated in previous chapters. With that in mind, here are some ideas to support using audiobooks in classrooms, libraries (both school and public), and home.

IN THE CLASSROOM

Elementary School—Grades K–5

ENGLISH LANGUAGE ARTS

Read Across America—Green Eggs and Ham by Dr. Seuss is a natural selection for listening to on the annual March 2 program observing Seuss's birthday. The rhythm and rhyming of the story provides a nice segue to many English language arts topics. Students can also make a list, as they listen, of all the words they hear that rhyme—a fun and useful audiobook for this celebration. Target grades K–2.

The Arnold Lobel Collection, by Arnold Lobel—The gentle humor and simple vocabulary of the four beginning-to-read stories lend themselves to a weeklong Lobel marathon. Listening to one story a day, noting (on chart paper or a whiteboard) the general theme and plot details plus a brief discussion of the story each day can culminate on day 5 with a compare-and-contrast discussion of the four stories. Target grades K–1.

Lon Po Po, written and illustrated by Ed Young. This version of Red Riding Hood is set in China and can be used in a classroom setting for several activities. During a Caldecott Medal unit, use *Lon Po Po* as a vehicle to discuss the illustrations, to compare with other Caldecott Medal winners, and to listen to the narration as visual literacy skills are activated. When exploring different versions of Red Riding Hood, this audiobook is an excellent addition to the discussion about how this story differs and/or is the same. Fairy-tale and folktale units can also provide an opportunity to include the classic tale of Red Riding Hood and this award-winning adaptation. Students may also compare audio and print titles of many folktales, including this one. Target grades 1–3.

Alice's Adventures in Wonderland, by Lewis Carroll. Many students who listen to audiobooks are familiar with the remarkable narrator Jim Dale, who magically brought the Harry Potter books to a higher level with his vocal interpretations of every character. He has done the same with Alice, enhancing the humor and the fantastic of the world in Wonderland. Listening to this classic in the hands of a world-class performer will bring students appreciation of this age-old story. As students listen to a chapter or two a day, they can write a journal entry about the story, discuss how characteristics of people in Alice's Wonderland are like "real" people, or write a version of how they would react if they were to go down the rabbit hole. Target grades 3–5.

The Gardener, written by Sarah Stewart, illustrated by David Small. We have annotated several audiobooks for grades K–2 that could be a fine combination for both language arts and science activities. *The Gardener, Miss Bridie Chose a Shovel*, and *A Child's Calendar* all lend themselves to the study of story; use of language; and the human connection to the land, to growing, to the change in seasons. The class could complete a chart comparing and contrasting the three stories or creating a diagram that indicates overlapping themes. A natural activity to include with listening to these stories would be a class gardening project: rooting vegetables, growing seeds, creating a terrarium, planting a school outdoor garden—the options can be as simple or as broad ranging as a teacher's planning will allow.

HISTORY/SOCIAL STUDIES

Henry Hikes to Fitchburg, written and illustrated by D. B. Johnson. This audiobook provides a seamless introduction to many environment themes, from observing the natural world to enjoying the outdoors and even the benefits of exercise. Lessons can integrate with history and social studies, science, and English language arts, as Henry and his friend view their travels in very different ways. Students may keep a journal of the specific nature details they observe on their way to and from school, and the class can compare and contrast the observations. Target grades K–2.

The Birchbark House, by Louise Erdrich. During a unit on Native Americans, students can listen to the story as a class and take notes on the customs and culture. Class discussion topics could center on what is similar and different from today's world in relation to families, food, celebrations, and so on. How did the disease smallpox affect the tribe, and could such an epidemic happen today? As mentioned in the previous chapter, this story is told from the Native American perspective, so it can be easily compared to *Little House in the Big Woods* or other titles in the Laura Ingalls Wilder series. Target grades 4–5.

Lincoln: A Photobiography, by Russell Freedman. There are a number of excellent audiobook biographies for grades 4–5 that we have annotated in chapter 5 and that would be useful for a classroom exploration of famous people. Choose several biographies for groups of three to four students to listen to. Each group can prepare a report to present to the class, specifically noting details from the audiobook and possibly choosing an example for the class to listen to. Besides *Lincoln: A Photobiography*, other suggested biographies for this activity are *Action Jackson*, by Jan Greenberg; *March On! The Day My Brother Martin Changed the World*, written by Christine King Farris; *Reaching for the Moon*, by Buzz Aldrin; and *When Marian Sang*, by Pam Muñoz Ryan. The breadth of topics these represent range from presidential history to art, the civil rights movement, science and space exploration, and music. Target grades 4–5.

SCIENCE

Bear Snores On, by Karma Wilson. Young students enjoy play, and the topic of animal habitats can elicit a creative activity in the classroom. How many habitats can students list, what does the habitat look like, how would they create such a habitat, and would they be comfortable there? Imaginative play to create a cave, a nest, a den, and even a bed of leaves on the forest floor can make a hands-on demonstration of where animals live. Target grades K–1.

The Dinosaurs of Waterhouse Hawkins, by Barbara Kerley. Choosing a read-along is a familiar classroom strategy to elicit discussions on many topics, but choosing the just-right audiobook can add an important dimension. This example integrates science, fine arts, and biography. Featuring bold illustrations that the whole class can see, this story can easily be followed up with a discussion on dinosaurs, Hawkins's perseverance, art, and how his dinosaur sculptures increased scientific study of extinct animals—the options for this title are many. Target grades 2–4.

MATH

Caps for Sale: A Tale of a Peddler, Some Monkeys, and Their Monkey Business, written by Esphyr Slobodkina. Listening to this humorous story has made counting and sorting a fun activity. The audiobook can easily transition to a lesson or activity for grades K–1 on skills such as counting, sets, and classification.

Math Curse, written by Jon Scieszka. Disguised as a tongue-in-cheek exploration of mathematics, many calculations can be accomplished while listening to the story. The oversized illustrations also assist with the read-along format that includes music and sound effects. Students can strengthen skills in time and other hidden math objects while smiling at the comic format. Target grades 3–5.

Middle School, Grades 6–8

ENGLISH LANGUAGE ARTS

The Dark Is Rising, by Susan Cooper. The use of language in this award-winning title is distinguished and students could, while listening, note unfamiliar vocabulary words and look up definitions for an English language arts exercise. However, a number of Newbery, Sibert, and Odyssey stories could form a group listening activity. Students can choose which award title to read and/or listen to and then compare and contrast the differences between the performance and reading the print version. This supports literacy skills such as critical listening and comprehension. Some titles to consider besides *The Dark Is Rising* include *Elijah of Buxton*, by Christopher Paul Curtis (Newbery Honor), *Peace, Locomotion*, by Jacqueline Woodson (Newbery Honor), and *Claudette Colvin: Twice toward Justice*, by Phillip Hoose (Sibert Honor). Target grades 6–8.

The People Could Fly, by Virginia Hamilton. As mentioned in the previous chapter annotation, this collection of short stories is a natural for classroom use, tying African American culture to folktales. The excellent performance and the presentation format of classifying the story themes (animals, supernatural, fanciful, and freedom) provide rich opportunities for discussion, comparing and contrasting, audio production highlights, use of humor, and emotional impact of the stories. This title can be used during Black History Month and other history and social studies and English language arts units. Target grades 6–8.

Good Masters! Sweet Ladies! Voices from a Medieval Village, by Laura Amy Schlitz. The dramatic monologue format of the Newbery Medal–winning story pleads for a class presentation. After listening to the audiobook, students may choose which part to dramatize, varying the characters' voice and tone, examining the focus of each part carefully. A print copy of the story can offer opportunities for students to see how the interweaving of the story is presented. The listening followed by the opportunity to perform the story reinforces the underlying information about medieval life and culture. Target grades 6–8.

The Misfits, by James Howe. Middle school students will recognize the angst of the characters in this story—a collection of the young and disenfranchised who disguise their outsider status with courage and humor. The performance showcases the dialogue-based narrative with a full-cast production that brings the daily difficulties of middle school directly to the listener. After listening, this audiobook could be used for individual or small group reports, journal entries, or reflections on how the story represents the themes of racism, bullying, propaganda, and stereotyping, certainly fertile ground for discussion and problem solving. Students will be intrigued that this story is written by the same author of the popular and familiar Bunnicula series. Target grades 6–8.

SCIENCE

Charles and Emma: The Darwins' Leap of Faith, by Deborah Heiligman. Scientific inquiry and biography are seamlessly integrated in this 2010 Newbery Honor and 2010 Michael L. Printz Honor Book—certainly a distinguished story of the Darwins' work and marriage. The audiobook performance gives a period tone that engages listeners to research more about the Darwins. Coincidentally, another 2010 Newbery Honor title, *The Evolution of Calpurnia Tate*, by Jacqueline Kelly, is an excellent listening combination, not only for science but also for English language arts. Students may take notes while listening to both titles and participate in a classroom discussion that reflects their ideas on how both stories relate the contributions of Charles and Emma Darwin. Target grades 6–8.

High School: Grades 9–12

ENGLISH LANGUAGE ARTS

The Absolutely True Story of a Part-Time Indian, by Sherman Alexie. The power of this multiple-award-winning story is the author's outstanding narration. Who else could bring the humor, pathos, and courage of Junior's story to the listener? Who else but Alexie himself, not only a prolific writer but an award-winning poet, too. His biography, on which this story is based, provides fertile ground for student exploration of his other works and topics for discussion. His themes of Native American reservation life, alcoholism, family, prejudice, and resilience offer students a rich collection of ideas for writing, reflection, and class reports. Target grades 11–12.

The Call of the Wild, by Jack London. Many lists of classic American literature include this early-twentieth-century title. The universal theme of survival is strengthened by this audiobook production and narration, and the vocal performance brings fresh energy to the listener. Students today will not feel that this tale is dated, because Buck's story is timeless. A unit that includes classic stories can assign lessons to analyze the language, plot, and literary effects that are demonstrated in *The Call of the Wild.* Target grades 9–10.

Hamlet, by William Shakespeare. During a unit on Shakespeare, students can take parts of the play and compare and contrast reading the text with the dramatic performance in the audio version—students can also cite specific details, such as tone and pacing of the narration. Questions such as "Does the audiobook version give fuller meaning to Shakespeare's words?" can be discussed. Play specific tracks that feature critical scenes and examine the emotion, language, and vocabulary. Target grades 10–12.

HISTORY/SOCIAL STUDIES

The Boy Who Dared and *Hitler Youth: Growing Up in Hitler's Shadow,* by Susan Campbell Bartoletti. Both award-winning titles focus on Hitler's Nazi Germany during World War II. The nonfiction title demonstrates a current trend in audiobook publishing, producing informational texts that often include bonus CDs with photographs, maps, and other graphic images. It is an interesting exercise to listen to *Hitler Youth* and not see the photographs of the young people until afterward—making the impact of the narrative much stronger. A class discussion comparing and contrasting the similarities and differences between the two stories—one fiction and one nonfiction—can feature the important issues that were imposed on German youth during the Hitler regime. Target grades 9–10.

The Three Documents That Made America: The Declaration of Independence, the Constitution of the U.S.A., and the Bill of Rights. This audiobook presents the founding philosophy of the United States in a compelling manner, a performance by a professional narrator. Classes in U.S. history and government can benefit from using the audiobook to bring to life the emotion and resolve of the revolutionary patriots. The narration gives the prose its due and provides an impetus for students to analyze the ideas and philosophy represented in those words.

Students may write individual or small-group reports on each document and present their opinions of how the audiobook heightens the meaning and comprehension of the Constitution, Bill of Rights, and Declaration of Independence. Target grades 10–12.

THEATER AND DRAMA

Harry Potter and the Half-Blood Prince (Book 6), *Harry Potter and the Deathly Hallows (Book 7)*, by J. K. Rowling. Many high school students will be familiar with the Harry Potter series, and as mentioned in chapter 5, the first book, *Harry Potter and the Sorcerer's Stone*, is accessible for grades 4–5. However, as Harry's story progresses, the themes and events turn more mature, so that by these last two books, listening is appropriate for older students. The extraordinary performance by Jim Dale provides a fine opportunity for theater and drama students to listen to and study his range of vocal characterizations and to list and discuss Dale's remarkable voicing of multiple characters in the last two titles. *Deathly Hallows* won a 2008 Odyssey Honor, the first year the awards were presented. In the classroom, several chapters can demonstrate important dramatic skills as students listen and discern Dale's differentiation of Harry, Hermione, Ron, and Hagrid, as well as various other characters. A class discussion should elicit interesting perspectives about how narrators and actors create, through their vocal interpretations, each individual personality.

IN THE SCHOOL LIBRARY MEDIA CENTER

Professional Outreach to Teaching Staff

In a regularly published school library newsletter, list new audiobook titles that are available for checkout.

In curriculum-based bibliographies, include audiobook titles by subject and theme.

For contributions to parent-teacher newsletters, list audiobook suggestions for families to listen to together.

Grades K–5

During specific monthly observances create an audiobook display or showcase that features titles connected to the celebration: Black History Month (*Bud, Not Buddy, Blues Journey, March On!*), Women's

History Month (*What to Do about Alice, Players in Pigtails, Rosa*), School Library Media Month (award-winning audiobooks: *Louise, the Adventures of a Chicken, Martina, the Beautiful Cockroach, Dooby, Dooby, Moo*), and National Poetry Month (*Love That Dog, Red Sings from Treetops, Green Eggs and Ham*). There are numerous possibilities for celebrating audiobooks.

Provide audiobook lessons to whole classes. A variation of the traditional story time, an audiobook can be chosen, depending on the grade level, to highlight how an excellent narration can increase the enjoyment of a story. Examples are *Knuffle Bunny*, which totally engages young listeners with Mo and Trixie Willems telling the story themselves, and *When Marian Sang*, an inspiring story that makes the impact of her talent compellingly evident when listeners hear her voice.

Battle of the Audiobooks is a monthlong event, another variation of a familiar library activity. Students may choose an audiobook to listen to and prepare a brief oral presentation giving the positive points of the story and narration. Classes can vote on which audiobook they would most like to listen to. A library display of audiobook titles and scorecard of voting can make this an inviting introduction to audiobooks.

Middle School: Grades 6–8

If the school has a daily or weekly closed-circuit television broadcast, student reporters or volunteers can write a review for an audiobook they have enjoyed and would recommend to their friends. This review can be televised to the school. Word of mouth by students is often a successful way to increase audiobook listening.

For technology instruction, use audiobooks as a springboard for a discussion of technology trends, such as whether participants prefer CDs, MP3s, or downloads and why. Teenagers are often early adopters of technology and frequently listen to audiobooks. The lesson and discussion can also include hands-on demonstrations of how to download an audiobook to a computer or MP3 player.

In January the annual awards for children's and young adult literature are announced. The Odyssey Award for Excellence in Audiobook Production was inaugurated in 2008 and the medal-winning and honor titles offer some memorable stories performed by the best narrators. Playing excerpts of these winning audiobooks can initiate an increase in requests from students. The 2011 Odyssey Medal winner, *The True Meaning of Smekday*, by Adam Rex, is a surefire introduction to the world of audiobooks and a fine example of a story rising to further excellence with the incredible performance by Bahni Turpin.

One of the best moments working with young people is the introduction of a good story, and there are many audiobooks that truly engage the listener, right from the beginning. When the story is fresh, something that has just been published, and no word of mouth has been generated yet, students discover the story and the performance while it is new. We have seen a group of students gathered around a CD player, ready to hear the first chapter of a new title, without one sound in the library except the story, performed beautifully by the narrator. This proves to be a goal all by itself, listening to the language, the vocabulary, and the fluency of the performance, and the result is often enthusiastic listeners who want to know what happens and, in that process, enhance their listening and comprehension skills.

In my middle-school library, I have begun to teach explicit audiobook listening skills in a single class period. I start with a large display of my favorite audiobooks, pairing a few with the print title. I share with the class the discovery of my personal listening style. I list a variety of audiobook listening station options:

Listening on the computer while watching the Media Player visualization, playing one of the basic Windows games such as Solitaire or Minesweeper, or drawing using Microsoft Paint.

Listening on a portable CD player while seated at a table and drawing.

Listening in one of the library's comfy chairs, either with print book in hand or not.

Listening while sprawled on the floor, with an optional eye bag made from a pantyhose sock and navy beans to block light.

Students choose an audiobook and spend the rest of the class period listening. The result? Amazed students who comment, "I thought you had to read while you listen," "I didn't know I could understand a book just by listening," and "It's so awesome how I can hear the story while doing something else!" I end the class by encouraging students to find their own listening style and remarking that I wish we had an exercise bike, Play-Doh, or knitting to try. I ask if any students want to check out their audiobook—and more than half the class will leave with audiobook in hand. Some of the most enthusiastic converts to audiobooks are gifted readers who, prior to this exercise, thought that listening was just for those with reading difficulties. In the words of a book-a-day eighth grader, "Listening slowed me down and let me relax. I revisited a book I had read in print and discovered whole new parts of the story while listening. I can't wait to go back and listen to some of my old favorites!"[1]

—Mary Burkey, "Voices in My Head: Long-Form Listening," *Book Links* (July 2009, pp. 26–27)

High School: Grades 9–12

Assignments for classic literature can offer opportunities to compare the print version with a modern narration. In print for more than 125 years, *Treasure Island,* by Robert Louis Stevenson, was produced as an audiobook in 2007 and received a 2008 Odyssey Honor. Jim Hawkins and Long John Silver have never had their words spoken more dramatically than with Alfred Molina's narration. If students struggle with the nineteenth-century language and style, this audiobook will permit them to enjoy the story to its fullest. Introduce classics by playing selected excerpts from this stellar production.

Three excellent audiobooks can give students a perspective of the Civil War, World War I, and World War II. *A Savage Thunder,* by Jim Murphy, is the only nonfiction title suggested here, but it flows like a story, focusing on the Battle of Antietam. *Private Peaceful,* by Michael Morpurgo, is a novel set in World War I, and *The Book Thief,* by Marcus Zusak is set during World War II. This powerful trio could be introduced with excerpts during a library research project on the causes, impact, and personal sacrifices that war brings.

An introduction to the life and works of Ernest Hemingway can feature two audiobooks, *Ernest Hemingway: A Writer's Life,* by Catherine Reef, and *The Old Man and the Sea,* by Hemingway himself. The production of *The Old Man and the Sea* is especially fine, and students will learn much about the author's life from Reef's biography. As students begin an author study, excerpts from both audiobooks would be useful for students to begin taking notes for their research.

To give relief from the high school pressure cooker, even with some titles that are targeted for younger audiences, a humor-filled listening station is sure to have the high school crowd lining up. Be prepared for a few guffaws in the library. Suggested titles include *Sleeping Freshmen*

Never Lie, by David Lubar; *Knucklehead,* by Jon Scieszka; and *The True Meaning of Smekday,* by Adam Rex.

Public Library

Here we would like to make mention of our commitment to the roles of school and public librarians and their work with young people. We feel that there are many opportunities for library professionals to collaborate with one another even though their work settings are very different. Most activities in this section are programs that public librarians have provided, but we also highlight several projects and activities that we have worked on that feature both public and school librarians working together for the benefit of young people.

COLLABORATIVE PROFESSIONAL DEVELOPMENT EVENTS AND ACTIVITIES

Audiobook publisher panel discussion—Public and school librarians attended a half-day workshop that featured a panel of audiobook producers and publishers. The information and follow-up discussion presented the scenarios of how an audiobook title is acquired, how it is produced, and the process of studio recording. Response to this professional development activity was an awareness of audiobook materials and increased motivation to advocate for audiobook materials in both school and public libraries.

"Listening for Literacy: Audioliterature and Teen Readers"—This all-day workshop on adolescent literacy, funded by a grant through the Library Services and Technology Act, was a true collaboration. Public, school, and university librarians created informational sessions on audiobook evaluation, investigation of the link between audiobook listening and developing twenty-first-century skills; title pairings with specific instructional standards; a demonstration by an audiobook director and teen actors; and a panel of teen listeners who detailed why, what, and how audiobooks play a part in their lives. Also included was statistical information on teen listeners from an Audio Publishers Association representative and a booktalk on audiobooks and reading for pleasure. One high school librarian declared, "[It's] the best workshop I've ever attended!"

Summer reading lists—Collaboration between public and school librarians and English language arts staff was fostered by an annual selection of summer reading lists for middle school. A few meetings resulted in grade-level lists for assigned reading. This advance planning allowed the public library to purchase multiple copies and prepare displays to highlight the availability of books for summer reading assignments. Audiobooks of the summer titles were also listed, and listening to the audiobook fulfilled the required assignment. Both school and public librarians found that this preparation resulted in good responses from students and families for the summer reading assignment.

ELEMENTARY SCHOOL

Storytime programming—The range of audiobooks that can be used for elementary age storytime programming depends only on the type of story that is used. So many fine audiobooks are now available for group listening that it is difficult to choose an example. A longtime favorite is *Charlie Needs a Cloak*, by Tomie dePaola. The music, sound effects, and inherent comedy will have children engaged in this wonderful listening experience.

Parent and child readers' advisory—Parents visiting with their young children have many requests for suggested titles and stories for children. Eager listeners enjoy the comfort of a series of books, and the audiobooks of the Magic Tree House series, by Mary Pope Osborne, are a good recommendation.

Celebrations—Halloween, Valentine's Day, and Chinese New Year are only a few of the observances and celebrations that public library staff design during the year. Children's Day/Book Day (El día de los niños/El día de los libros) is a special opportunity to highlight children's books. An excellent audiobook that fits the occasion well is *Celia Cruz: Queen of Salsa*, by Veronica Chambers. With background salsa music, the life of the Cuban singer is an energetic and happy selection to use for group programming.

Author and narrator appearance—This public library programming event can also take place in a school setting, but scheduling is often easier in a public library, so that a performance or appearance can be in the evening or on a weekend. When authors are promoting a new book, they often travel across the country and will make a library appearance for minimal or no cost. There are also many local and regional authors who enjoy visiting with children. One interesting program is to have an audiobook narrator share with families how the narration is accomplished in the studio, as well as preparation, vocalization, and so on.

There are numerous variations of a special appearance that can highlight audiobooks.

MIDDLE SCHOOL

Teen Advisory Board (TAB) or Talking about Books or Teens and Books—This program has a number of nationwide examples, and it is how we met, one public librarian and one school librarian collaborating to work with students and advocate reading. The setting varies, at lunchtime, after school, even before school, but grade-level groups of students meet twice a month to talk about the books they are reading. The innovative part of the program that was developed featured students reading advance reader's copy young adult fiction that publishers had sent for preview. The incentive, to eager young readers, was to have the chance to read something even before it was published! The students were required to give formal feedback to the TAB sponsors (that was us, the school and public librarian) about their considered opinions about the book, not just the plot, characters, and so on. As the audiobook industry flourished, so did TAB's interest in listening to the latest stories, and students had the firsthand chance to read or listen and to compare and contrast the experience. This assisted in building critical listening skills, analyzing audio performance, and assessing whether the story worked well in either or both formats. Our middle school students made comparisons between the experience of reading "with their ears" or reading "with their eyeballs" (their terminology, not ours). As listening became more popular with students, we learned that when building an audiobook collection, an awareness of format preference and availability is important.

HIGH SCHOOL

High school students who are assigned classics in English language arts can appreciate other versions of stories, such as the audiobook or movie of *A Tree Grows in Brooklyn*. A library display of media adaptations of well-known stories can elicit interest in listening to audiobooks that represent fine performances. Other suggested stories are *The Whale Rider, The Fellowship of the Ring, Treasure Island,* and *The Old Man and the Sea*.

High School Teen Advisory Board (TAB)—As with the middle school TAB example, there are a number of high school TAB variations around the country. One we are familiar with is held at the public library in the evening. The book discussions also include audiobook listening, and the lure of pizza and good talk draws many teenagers to the monthly meetings.

Author studies and displays—High school students have many assignments that focus on authors of both classic and modern works. A library display that features a specific author's work, biographies, audiobooks, and reviews can attract listeners to learn more about the writer. Two examples that could be used for this library outreach are Sylvia Plath and Chris Crutcher. *Your Own, Sylvia* is a wonderful fictionalized audiobook biography to display with other Plath works. *King of the Mild Frontier: An Ill-Advised Autobiography,* by Chris Crutcher, is a superb audiobook introduction to the life of the popular young adult author. Students will be drawn to investigate more about these authors through such displays.

At Home

Ideas for student assignments—Nonfiction audiobooks have grown in availability, production quality, and performance. Students who have research, term papers, and/or assignments on specific topics in history and social studies, English language arts, science, and math might consider these audiobooks for good information: *Snowflake Bentley,* by Jacqueline Briggs Martin; *Anne Frank Remembered,* by Miep Gies; *American Tall Tales,* by Mary Pope Osborne; *Under the Blood Red Sun,* by Graham Salisbury; *To Kill a Mockingbird,* by Harper Lee; and *Troy,* by Adèle Geras. All of these audiobooks can support student learning and will be especially effective in allowing less able readers to access information on the same topics as their peers with higher degrees of reading proficiency.

Listening together as a family and during travel—There are innumerable audiobooks that can be enjoyed as a family or individually with those omnipresent earbuds. Listening to an audiobook can give personal enjoyment to families and often leads to lively discussion. Favorite stories, series, and classics can be listened to at home, in the car, or on vacation. Some suggested titles are *Winnie the Pooh,* by A. A. Milne; *Alice's Adventures in Wonderland,* by Lewis Carroll; *Charlotte's Web,* by E. B. White; *Because of Winn Dixie,* by Kate DiCamillo; and, of course, the Harry Potter series, narrated by the incomparable Jim Dale.

Sync: YA Listening—An innovative summer program was inaugurated in 2010 that attracted many teenagers to the audiobook format. Created and sponsored by *AudioFile* magazine, two audiobook titles were made available each week as free downloads. Carefully selected, the audiobooks paired contemporary and classic titles such as *Bloody Jack* with *Treasure Island,* and Suzanne Collins's wildly popular *The Hunger Games* with Shirley Jackson's *The Lottery.* The response was excellent, online dialogue was active at the newly created Audiobook Community, and future plans include an expanded list of pairings once again including classic and contemporary titles that appear on middle and high school summer reading lists (seewww.audiobookcommunity .com/group/sync).

Sync: YA Listening is a teen-listening book club that coordinates summer reading programs at libraries and schools with free-download audiobooks. Beginning in summer 2010, and offered through www .audiobookcommunity.com, the program builds the audience for YA audio by facilitating the discovery of the audiobook experience through free downloads and social networking.

Sync engages teens with language and storytelling in favored media—the MP3 players and phones that are essential tools of their lives. Two new books are offered weekly—one likely on the "official" summer reading list and the other on the teen's own reading list. Sync has excited both teens and summer reading program directors.

Audiobooks have a natural place in the busy lives of teens. The portable format and intimate, dynamic storytelling are two key features that draw in young adults. They love the personalities that come alive regardless of reading level and even engage with classics without the roadblocks that can deter teens from world lit.

—Robin Whitten, editor and publisher of *AudioFile* magazine
(Sync: YA Listening is the brainchild of Jennifer Dowell Whitten and Kirsten Cappy; visit www.audiobookcommunity.com)

9

Technology Innovation Supports Audiobook Use

Who could have imagined the lightning speed of technology progression since the mid-1980s? Teachers and librarians have depended on audiovisual equipment in educational settings for many years, and the development of this equipment closely follows the growth of audiobooks for instructional use. The changes in listening equipment have had implications not only for budgeting in school and public libraries but also for storage, circulation, and portability. In this chapter, we briefly explore how audiobook formats have developed and how they have affected the listening experience.

The twenty-first century has brought images of young people connected to the digital world, in which technology changes faster than the turn of an e-book page. One only has to ride a public transportation system to see many people listening to their MP3 players—an important consideration, especially when realizing that there are digital natives among us! According to the Berkman Center for Internet and Society at Harvard University, there is a "generation 'born digital'—those who grow up immersed in digital technologies, for whom a life fully integrated with digital devices is the norm. By understanding young people's interactions with digital media . . . we may address the issues their practices raise, [and] learn how to harness the opportunities their digital fluency presents."[1] It is these digital natives who have their earbuds with them at all times and who especially enjoy listening to audiobooks. Those portable devices now have a cool factor, as they keep the listener in tune with current digital formats and up to date with the latest titles. But in school and public libraries, it wasn't always so. Audiobook platforms and designs have truly come a very long way.

> What I love most about audiobooks is that they are carrying on the long and honored oral tradition of storytelling. This is where stories started—being told. And how convenient that we don't have to carry around a storyteller. We can carry an iPod or a phone.
>
> —Jon Scieszka, children's book author and 2008 Library of Congress Ambassador for Young People's Literature

THE CASSETTE

Even though sound recordings of books had been available before the 1980s, cumbersome equipment, lack of production and sound quality, and flat vocal interpretations made the medium a poor substitute for live readings in a classroom or library. All this changed when the audiocassette and the audiocassette player and recorder were introduced in the early 1970s. Although this equipment might appear quaint in hindsight, it was a breakthrough for audiobook listening. It was the cassette tape and player that brought portability, ease of use, and cost efficiency to large numbers of users.

The cassette tape (quarter-inch magnetic) itself was encased in plastic and formed a loop that ran over a magnetic head. For classroom use, this development brought reliable sound reproduction to enhance instructional themes. Teachers and librarians could have a recorded story available at a moment's notice. Of course, in the beginning because the format was new, each school classroom did not have its own cassette player, so sharing was the norm. School and public library budgets often lag behind other institutions in the adoption of new equipment, especially because the record player (remember them?) was still in use. Those who used the cassette tape for audiobook listening quickly learned to appreciate its effective features, and before long audiobook publishers increased their title lists to support increased usage. In school settings, the cassette tape was used for both large group and individual listening. A single student could enjoy a story (with headphones), or a whole class could listen to a chapter during language arts. Listening stations in public libraries were installed, and some public libraries actually loaned out the equipment. Hand in hand with the adoption of the cassette tape and player as a mainstream format for audiobooks were continued performance and production improvement.

THE CASSETTE PLAYER AND RECORDER

The first cassette players were nondescript in their plastic cases and fairly large and cumbersome. Most audiovisual equipment follows the big-to-small continuum, so it wasn't long before cassette players were very light and portable and included a built-in carrying handle. The medium for listening to audiobooks became more convenient, an important consideration for school and public libraries.

The development of the combined audiocassette player and recorder allowed for dual use, making the piece of equipment a standard for schools. As the players and recorders became more popular, classroom teachers, especially in elementary schools, were pleased that each room had one of its own—no more sharing! Listening stations were set up with a cassette player, headphones attached with a jack, and—voilà—a student could listen to an audiobook. An example of how the advancement of the equipment led to increased instructional use was demonstrated by the presence of tape players in most schools and classrooms. They were inexpensive and easy to repair (school librarians knew how to clean the heads, untwist and splice the tape, and keep the equipment in good condition). School systems that had equipment technicians devised a summer maintenance program that kept the players in good working order.

By the 1990s, cassette tape players were commonly found in public libraries, in homes, and in schools. The only complaint concerning the equipment was the lack of compatibility between manufacturers; each player had the same controls, Play, Rewind, Fast-Forward, Record, Stop, Volume, and Pause, but every player was configured differently, so users could easily be confused about how a particular one worked. This difficulty was not particular to cassette players, because it is the norm with many types of equipment—an ongoing frustration for those who use and depend on consistency and reliability.

THE HANDHELD CASSETTE PLAYER

In the late 1970s a revolutionary format was introduced, the handheld cassette player, showcased by the Sony Walkman. Quickly recognized as a major solution to portability, the personal stereo cassette player became the most popular way to listen to music and audiobooks and was adopted by many manufacturers. Exercising, commuting on public transportation, at the beach, or on the patio, the handheld cassette player became ubiquitous. Users of all ages enjoyed being able to listen to a good story or their favorite music in privacy. The personal stereo was an individual format and was not used in schools or public libraries, but it paved the way for many future forms of personal listening.

HEADPHONES

Brief mention should be made about portable headphones, even though they had been available for many years before cassette players. The connection to the cassette tape player made the listening more personal and offered a more intimate experience—the story was being read just to one person. Headphones were oversized, heavy, and cumbersome, but like cassette tape players, they became smaller and smaller, allowing for more comfort while listening. For school and library budgets, headphones became an inexpensive accessory, and this encouraged audiobook use.

THE AUTOMOBILE CASSETTE PLAYER

In the mid-1970s cassette players were introduced into automobiles—the audiobook could easily travel, and stories came alive as the miles piled up. Families traveling on vacation and carpooling children to activities, commuters with long drives to work, business people who travel distances between clients—all adopted the audiocassette as a wonderful companion. Instead of trying to locate local radio stations, car travel could now include an audiobook: a classic, a biography, a funny or a sad story. And, as mentioned in chapter 1, the increased quality of audiobook performance and production made the listening experience in the car a positive for the publishing community. Who could resist listening today to *Harry Potter and the Sorcerer's Stone* performed by the award-winning Jim Dale? The car audiotape player was a major development for audiobook use. By the early twenty-first century, students could listen to summer reading assignments at home, on a bus, on the sub-way, or in the car, making availability and convenience commonplace, as well as accepted by most educators as "counting" for the assignment. During summer vacations and holidays, public library circulation for audiobooks increases dramatically as families travel—listening to a great story makes the miles go faster.

THE COMPACT DISC

Just as most audiobook listeners were getting familiar and comfortable with portable cassette players and the innovation of car players was widely available, a new format option came onto the scene, the compact disc. Along with the expansion and growth of computers, the digitization of data, and the continued miniaturization of technology, the CD was a concept that stretched the imagination. Hundreds and thousands of digital bits could be compressed onto a plastic disc—information, pictures, sound—truly an amazing transition that further enhanced audiobook possibilities. Because the digital data could be placed in smaller space than on a magnetic cassette tape, a whole book that previously took eight tapes could be manufactured on four CDs.

This advance changed many features for audiobook publishers—portability, reliability, and that elusive cool factor. Even though CDs scratch pretty easily, magnetic desensitizers cannot erase them. Much of the maintenance was limited to keeping the surface of the CD clean. The shiny-mirror surface and Frisbee-like appearance cloaked the sturdy dependability of the audio recording, unless warping from high heat or breakage as a result of impact occurred. The CD quickly overtook the cassette tape as the delivery mechanism for audiobooks.

All of this does not discount the continued presence of cassette tapes in some homes and classrooms, especially the read-along format. The small cassette tape and player is a comfortable solution for many, and a few audio publishers continue to provide this choice. However, most public and school libraries are phasing out the cassette tape option for their patrons.

THE COMPACT DISC PLAYER

Along with the introduction of the CD came another excellent innovation, the equipment to play the CDs. Even with the portable cassette player becoming widespread in earlier years, the adoption of small CD players, such as the Sony Discman, synchronized with the increasing growth of technology formats in general. As computers became the norm in schools and libraries, so did the improvement of audiobook production. The CD player used laser light to read the digital information and compressed the book into millions of bits. Initially, there were some difficulties with pausing a CD, locating the exact spot where the listening stopped, and so on. This was eventually resolved with distinct tracking that helped with planned and unexpected interruptions in listening.

By the beginning of the twenty-first century, CD players were already encroaching on the continued use of cassette players. Even with budget constraints, school and public libraries purchased CD players for whole-group and individual listening. Teachers could easily use an audiobook on CD as a class listening experience. Thankfully, the features of the CD players were consistent with cassette players, so users could easily learn how to operate the equipment.

Individual audiobook listeners could enjoy a story on a small portable CD player and teenagers especially liked the idea of carrying audiobooks along with them.

Circulation of audiobooks has continued to increase as the technology became accessible, affordable, and dependable. The CD player followed the cassette tape player into automobiles, so much so that, in the early twenty-first century, cassette players were no longer offered in cars. In schools and libraries, both CDs and cassette players overlapped use for many years, even though the CD was eventually the universally accepted format for audiobook listeners.

STORAGE OF AUDIOBOOK COLLECTIONS

School and public libraries frequently have storage questions when new materials are developed, and the arrival of audiobooks, whether conformed as a book alone, a cassette tape–book or a CD-book initially presented a challenge. How would this package be shelved, how would it be cataloged? As a book? A tape? An audiobook? Would they be separately categorized or intershelved with regular materials? Thankfully, audiobook publishers and library supply vendors quickly devised a number of systems to display, protect, and shelve audiobooks, including plastic hangers, metal clothesline racks, and other choices to help store audiobook collections. These display options made audiobook choices more visible and attractive to students and library patrons.

PRINT AND AUDIOBOOK PUBLICATION RELEASES

Another factor in audiobook use has been the simultaneous publication of audio and print editions. Readers and listeners can choose which format they prefer, print or audio. Conversely, when audiobooks were first published for school and public library consumption, the title often was months, even years, away from the print publication. That detail could be both a plus and a minus—with the separation of publication, listening to an audiobook was like rediscovering a favorite. The success of the audiobook publishing industry has also caused many older titles to be produced, making the rediscovery of great stories even more visible.

THE MP3 PLAYER AND THE IPOD

A digital audio player (DAP), commonly called an MP3 player (or personal digital player), is able to compress music and audio files in a very small format. In 2001, the Apple Corporation released its first version of their MP3 player, the iPod. Another milestone in design and use, the iPod has changed the face of the audiobook interface, resulting in the subway and bus earbud syndrome mentioned earlier. As fast as a new technology is adopted, it changes, so again, the speed of technology innovation affects audiobook production. Now, MP3 players have been miniaturized to the size of your palm and weigh less than ever. Travelers, students, commuters, and most teenagers are connected to their iPods in a way that has personalized the audiobook listening experience. Even as MP3 players have become ubiquitous, the arrival of smartphones has added another portable interface for audiobook listening. With the flick of the wrist, headphones are attached, and the combined cell phone, MP3 player, and Internet interface is ready to go. Listening to the best in audiobook production has never been easier.

THE PLAYAWAY

The progression of audiobook delivery systems has evolved from analog to digital, from tabletop to handheld, and from cassettes to CDs to the Playaway. Introduced as a preloaded digital audio player, this easy-to-use, compact, all-inclusive device has gained wide acceptance in school and public libraries. As the Playaway advertisement says, "No Cassettes, No CDs, No Downloads, Just Play."

When Playaway first became available, I was intrigued but wary. Who would use them? To what extent? How sturdy are they? What about security issues? Are they worth the extra cost? I bought a few titles as an experiment. To say it was successful is an understatement. Today, our library display of Playaway selections is more empty than full throughout the school year because of the huge popularity of this format among our students. Word-of-mouth promotion means that I actually have to do very little publicity; the kids tell each other and their teachers . . . and the Playaways fly off the shelves. Teachers have welcomed this format because of its appeal to struggling and reluctant readers, as well as to the more proficient ones. Playaway is cool . . . and it counts as real reading!

—Mary Stump, library media specialist,
Kenmore Middle School, Arlington, Virginia

Durability, ease of circulation and wide range of title selection offsets the higher price of the Playaway format, even in constrained budget times. Especially for students who do not have access to an MP3 player, the Playaway is a terrific substitute. It's about the same size as an MP3 player, easily fits in your pocket, and it definitely has that cool factor. It's also perfect for those who don't have high-level tech skills or access to a computer for downloading audiobooks because you just put in the battery, plug in your earbuds, and you're ready to go with a wonderful story. In a school environment the Playaway can be shared with a whole class by connecting it to a set of speakers or to a docking station. This is also true for the iPad and iPod.

SATELLITE RADIO

Another consideration is the advent of satellite radio subscription services, such as XM Sirius Radio. There are channels that showcase audiobooks, such as Radio Classics, in which original productions of classics (e.g., Edgar Allan Poe, Sherlock Holmes) are performed with a full cast. A number of audiobook publishers also announce their new releases on satellite radio. Listeners can learn about featured audiobooks if they have access to this nationwide service. Although satellite radio is not readily available in the classroom, it does provide another avenue for students to listen to audiobooks.

ONLINE LIBRARY CATALOGS

The evolution of technology advancement that has supported the availability of audiobooks also includes the development of online library catalogs. From the on-site paper catalogs that contained many drawers of information to today's digital format, library catalogs are available to all listeners with the click of a mouse. The presentation of information clearly gives format options for all titles, so from school, at home, or in the public library, audiobooks are clearly visible to indicate availability. This is just another innovation that has affected the use of audiobooks in instructional settings.

DOWNLOADING AUDIOBOOKS

Audiobooks through an MP3 player can be downloaded in minutes via a computer, which then synchronizes to the MP3 player. For digital natives, this is an easy process—manipulation of technology is second nature to them. For other users, downloading can be confusing, given the different protocols of various delivery platforms. In talking with both school and public librarians, it is apparent that the current status of free downloading of audiobooks through a subscription service—made possible via the online catalog—is available mainly at the public library, as school libraries have not had the capability or the budget resources to purchase this kind of service. This does provide a fine opportunity for collaboration between school and public librarians—each student who has a public library card is able to access an OverDrive account or other subscription-based library-provided resources. For those who want to build their own collection of audiobooks, services such as Audible or iTunes provide downloads, and the breadth of titles available continues to grow. And yes, feather-light computer tablets, such as the iPad, have once again provided another technology device for audiobook delivery. The touch features of the iPad make downloading even faster because the digital processors run at lightning speeds. Is the digital format the final choice for audiobook access, and will the CD become less popular? Let us explore what might be next in the technology to deliver audiobooks.

WHAT IS NEXT?

One excellent resource for current audiobook recommendations, information, and what's hot and what's next in the world of audiobooks is

Mary Burkey's blog, *Audiobooker,* a regular feature of the American Library Association's *Booklist* online newsletter (http://audiobooker .booklistonline.com). As the chair of the inaugural Odyssey Award Committee, Burkey has her finger on the pulse of the audiobook world. One discussion point that she makes on how the audiobook will evolve is that forward-thinking formats have frequently emanated from the audiobook industry. A case in point is the digital download, begun by Audible in 1995 and followed by OverDrive a very long time before the current broad availability. Burkey predicts that the coming years will bring more integration of text, audio, and video and that the combined interface will attract more listeners to the audiobook experience.

Another source for what's next in audiobooks is *AudioFile* magazine, a bimonthly publication that not only reviews current titles but also features articles that give thoughtful viewpoints on new technology, how-tos for choosing audiobooks for a specific audience, and general information, which makes this a go-to journal for those wanting to learn more about the audiobook community.

CONCLUSION

One thing is certain: when it comes to an audiobook delivery system, the critical and important feature is the core of the material, the story. Listening to the story is what gives the listener the experience and the tradition of storytelling, and the story is what brings all listeners to the best that can be recorded, whether on a cassette, a CD, or a digital download. As the audiobook industry has grown from cassette tape to CD and then downloads, the production techniques and performance have also grown. From a straightforward atonal narration to some of today's top performers, the core of the audiobook still remains the story, and the story brings the best in human creativity to all listeners.

NOTE

1. Berkman Center for Internet and Society at Harvard University, "Digital Natives," http://cyber.law.harvard.edu/research/digitalnatives.

10

Finding the Best

W e've recommended many titles we think work well in classroom, library, and home settings, and now it's time to point you to the places where you can continue to find excellent audiobooks to share with young people. We list here the sources we use to build collections as well as to inform our own work with children, teens, and their families.

REVIEW SOURCES IN JOURNALS

Booklist magazine, published by the American Library Association, offers a wide range of recommended audiobook titles for children, teens, and adults, now in the issue that comes out the fifteenth of each month (January and June issues are combined). *Booklist* also produces an annual Editors' Choice list, published in January, that includes audio titles. The ALA notable lists (Notable Recordings for Children and Amazing Audiobooks for Young Adults are among these) can generally be found in the March 15 issue and audiobooks are often part of the Spotlight features. The magazine features Mary Burkey's "Voices in My Head" column on audiobooks four times per year. The online edition provides easy access to both current and past reviews as well as to the various *Booklist* blogs (see the information on Audiobooker later in this chapter) and articles. *Booklist* sponsors the annual Odyssey Award for Excellence in Audiobook Production, and its media editor serves as an invaluable consultant to the committee. *Booklist* publishes an in-depth interview with the Odyssey Award–winning producer each year. *Book Links*, a quarterly publication of *Booklist*, connects teachers, librarians, and others with thematic materials featuring "high-quality literature-based resources" for use in the classroom. *Book Links* has sometimes included articles on audiobooks for children in grades K–8.

AudioFile magazine, an independent journal that focuses exclusively on spoken word audio productions, features monthly reviews of audiobooks for children and family listening and young adults. Earphone Awards are given to those productions deemed especially noteworthy by reviewers, and there is an annual Best Audiobooks list. *AudioFile* also pioneered the Audiobooks on the Go list for student and family summer listening; it is published each April in the print edition, with expanded features online. Interviews with authors and narrators, as well other audiophiles, provide particular interest, especially for public library patrons.

School Library Journal provides monthly reviews written by school and public librarians and others on a wide range of audiobooks. Because most of the reviewers are practitioners who work directly with students, the age range suggestions are especially helpful for school and public library collection development. *School Library Journal* features many articles and columns each month that, though not focused on audiobooks, support the work of librarians in schools and public libraries. The journal also features our bimonthly column "ListenIn—Audiobooks and Learning." *Curriculum Connections*, a supplement of the journal, sometimes features articles on audiobooks as well as suggested titles for classroom use.

VOYA (Voice of Youth Advocates) magazine features a column on audiobooks by Teri Lesesne in the April, August, and December issues. In "AudioTalk," Lesesne offers information about teens and listening, as well as reviews of audiobooks with special appeal to teen listeners. A member of the inaugural Odyssey Award Committee, Lesesne teaches children's and young adult literature at Sam Houston State University in Texas, has written several books on literature and young adults, and is eminently qualified to recommend audiobook titles to teens and those who work with them.

Library Media Connection's column "Listen Up! What's New in Audiobooks" is written by longtime audiobook listener, Audies judge, and children's literature expert Jeanette Larson. Included in the August–September and December issues of the journal, this column focuses on using audiobooks with young people, reviewing new audiobook offerings, and information on industry trends.

BLOGS

Audiobooker, http://audiobooker.booklistonline.com, by Mary Burkey—Mary Burkey is a middle school librarian in suburban Columbus, Ohio, who has been using and evaluating audiobooks with students and colleagues for years. She has served on and chaired ALA's Notable Recordings for Children Committee and chaired the inaugural Odyssey Award Committee. Her blog includes information for teachers, librarians, and audiobook hounds. She also often dishes out fascinating facts from the audiobook industry, including interviews with producers and narrators. While you're there, check out the article "Why One English Teacher Values the Audiobook."

Reading with My Ears, www.readingwithmyears.blogspot.com, by Lee Catalano—Lee Catalano is a teen services librarian in Portland, Oregon, and provides fascinating, in-depth reviews of the latest audiobooks for children and teens. She has served on and chaired ALA's Amazing Audiobooks for Young Adults Committee and served on the 2010 Odyssey Award Committee. Her entertaining and informative style makes for interesting reading.

AWARDS AND BEST-OF LISTS

Odyssey Award for Excellence in Audiobook Production (www.ala.org/ala/mgrps/divs/alsc/awardsgrants/bookmedia/odysseyaward/)—This annual award is given to the producer of the best audiobook produced for children and/or young adults, available in English in the United States.

Amazing Audiobooks for Young Adults (www.ala.org/ala/mgrps/divs/yalsa/booklistsawards/amazingaudiobooks/audiobooks.cfm)—Each year, the Young Adult Library Services Association's Amazing Audiobooks Committee selects and annotates a list of notable audio recordings significant to young adults from titles released in the past two years.

Notable Children's Recordings (www.ala.org/ala/mgrps/divs/alsc/awards/grants/notalists/ncb/)—This annual list from the Association for Library Service to Children identifies the best of the best in children's recordings.

The Audie Awards (www.audiopub.org/index.asp)—These awards recognize distinction in audiobooks and spoken word entertainment and are sponsored by the Audio Publishers Association.

Capitol Choices: Noteworthy Books for Children and Teens (www .capitolchoices.org)—This site includes audiobooks in its annual list of outstanding titles for young people. Visit the website and enter "audiobooks" in the search box to see everything selected over the years, or click on one of the annual lists and click on the "Audiobooks" section.

NEWSPAPERS

Newspapers often have occasional columns featuring audiobooks, particularly for family listening. We've seen such articles in big newspapers such as the *Washington Post* but have also found columns in smaller, local papers.

Audiobook Lexicon

The following list was compiled and edited by Mary Burkey in July 2011 and originally printed in the October–November 2007 issue of *Audio-File* magazine. The following audio producers generously contributed to the creation of this list: Arnie Cardillo (Live Oak Media), Michele Cobb (AudioGo), Bruce Coville (Full Cast Audio), Tim Ditlow (Brilliance Audio), Todd and Brett Hobin (Hobin Studios), Paul Gagne (Weston Woods), Eileen Hutton (Brilliance Audio), Troy Juliar (Recorded Books), Pete Pantelis, and David Rapkin (David Rapkin Audio Production).

abridged   original work edited by professional abridger, with goal of staying true to spirit and content of book

accent   of a specific nationality or region, such as German or midwestern, or a socioeconomic or class accent

actuality audio   section of audio from another source (e.g., interviews, animal sounds) added to the original studio recording

ambience   sound quality that comes from the recording studio environment rather than directly from the sound source

attributives   identifying phrases such as "he said" and "she whispered"

audio cue mismatch   audio mismatch with source visual or text; a sound effect or added music that does not match the text or, in read-alongs, match the illustration

audiobook original   audiobook with no print or e-book counterpart, or a title that is available in audio before print or e-book publication

bonus material   extras added to audio title or items from print title that may be on audio (e.g., time line, glossary, author interview)

book app   interactive digital book that is accessed on a device such as a tablet computer or mobile phone and may include synchronized text, animations, audio, and more

break point   logical and appropriate stopping points of audio medium segments or other breaks in the audio production

breathy   type of mouth sound, sharp or odd breaths of narrator, audible breaths at sentence breaks

bright   sound quality that is clear and sharp

cadence   rhythm of speech created through modulation and inflection

choppy edit   noticeable or abrupt editing of sound

clam shell   hard case designed for multiple circulations and used for library and school editions of physical audiobooks

clarity of narration   clear and understandable reading and diction

clarity of production   recording clarity, clean sound throughout title, not muddy or muted

clipped edit   end of a word is cut off in audio editing

consistency   narrator maintaining energy and character voicings, even if narration was recorded at different times

context of line   maintaining meaning of text through expression and emphasis

continuous record   narration recorded in extended segments without interruption, as opposed to punch-in edits

cover art   audiobook may match hardcover or paperback print item's cover art or may be entirely different

cultural authenticity   match of reader and culture of character—accents or dialects authentic, not stereotyped; may include authentic music

dialect   of a specific group of people (e.g., Appalachian)

digital distortion   cracking or blurry sound when volume exceeds upper digital range

digital download   audiobook available as a digital file, accessed and downloaded directly to computer or playback device, needing no delivery medium

digital only   audiobooks distributed by a publisher solely as a download

director person hired to direct the talent in the studio during the audiobook recording

direct-to-consumer digital digital audiobooks that need no distribution media (e.g., MP3, CD, preloaded digital player) and are accessed by a playback device

distribution media method of delivering audio (MP3, preloaded digital player, CD) that requires another playback device such as a CD player

download service vendor an arrangement of an individual or library system to purchase licensed audiobooks from an Internet retailer (e.g. Audible, OverDrive)

dramatic dynamic range controlled range of volume, with emotion shown through energy, not resulting in uneven sound levels

dramatization adaptation, usually multivoiced, often with sound effects, music, and interaction; often called audio drama or radio theater (*not* same as multivoiced)

DRM digital rights management, technologies used by publishers or distributors that control access or usage of digital audio

dry mouth clicking mouth sound

emotion degree to which emotional content of text is expressed; explication of the meaning of text through the voice

energy a quality of narrator's reading that engenders listener engagement

enhanced product material added to audiobook package (e.g., illustrations, games, computer files, video); see also "value-added"

equalization pleasant and nonfatiguing tonal quality over full range of audio spectrum of audio format

executive producer person employed by audio publisher to oversee total audiobook production and funding

expression overall performance quality, using a range that engenders listener engagement

extras forewords, afterwords, glossaries, dedications, photo captions or notes, miscellaneous words that appear in picture book's illustrations

fades, in and out bringing in or out music and sound effects; may be gradual or steep; also known as ramping sounds in or out *flat*   narration that seems dull, unemotional, monotone

formatting   editing to fit on cassette (104 minute), CD (80 minute), or MP3-CD (more than 12 hours)

full-cast narration   multiple narrators performing as individual characters during ensemble reading

fully voiced   a single narrator using a range of multiple character differentiations and voicings in a solo performance

gluey   mouth sound

hardware   the physical device used to access an audio medium

hiss   audible background noise, unwarranted high-frequency noise

hollow   sound quality that echoes or lacks depth

hot sound   audio quality that is too loud or intense (i.e., hot)

ID3 tags   metadata that allow CD and digital audio players to display track and title information

incidental music   music at beginning, end, or other points in production

index points (track points)   invisible markings that allow listener to jump to points on audio file—may be of varied length, depending on producer

inflection   overall performance quality, rise and fall of voice pitch used for expression

intro   identifies title, author, narrator, and so on

juicy   wet type of mouth sound, saliva noise

licensed audiobook   audiobook available for legal purchase through authorized distributor by arrangement with the producer

lifeless   sound quality that does not engage the listener, dry

liner notes   text or visual material describing the production, may be printed on sleeve or wrap or available digitally

lip smacks   type of mouth sound

listener engagement   the involvement of the listener in the production

medium   a means that provides transmission or storage of information

missing text   errors in which text from source is missing in finished audio production

mix   combining distinct tracks or audio segments into a unified production *mood* emotional ambience of the audio, created by narrator's voice, music, and sound effects

mouth clicks type of mouth sound

MP3 audio encoding format that compresses data, used for downloaded audiobooks and for MP3-CDs that hold more than an eighty-minute CD

muddy sound quality—audio muffled, or indistinct; excess of bass energy, missing mid to high frequencies

multivoiced production more than one narrator but not necessarily an actor for each character or recorded as an ensemble at the same time

mushy vocal quality, lack of precision in diction

music cues (tags) music used to note scene change, identify character, depict mood, reference time period, or other aspect of production

music library stock music licensed from a vendor, used in the audiobook production

musical bed music that is heard under the voice, throughout portions or large parts of the production

musical intro music at beginning of production

musical outro music at end of production

narrator one who delivers the content of the audiobook

narrator match narrator voice matches character age, gender, time period, setting, mood, and so on

noisegating an abrupt edit resulting in clipped words or in silence between words

off mic narrator is recorded away from the microphone, or narrator's mouth turns away from the microphone

original music musical score that is composed expressly for the audiobook production

out of sync mismatched sound and visual, when the voice doesn't track with the visual in a production such as a read-along picture book

outro information at end of production, may contain program title, performer's name, author, publisher information, copyright, and so on

pacing of narration   narrator's reading too fast or too slow

pacing of production   passages paced correctly for dramatic arc of story

page rate   how long it takes a narrator to complete a page of text, also known as pickup or reader acquisition rate

page turn (paper noise)   studio noise

partially voiced   a single narrator using primarily a straight read, with a few major character differentiations

peaky   sound quality that is too high in sound or energy level

pitch range   high or low range of sound

playback device   hardware (e.g., iPod, cell phone, CD player) that allows playback of distribution media (e.g., cassette tape, CD) or digital files (e.g., MP3, WMA)

plosives or wind pops   noticeable microphone noise, mouth pop sounds; *p, t,* and *f* pops

podiobook   serialized, unpublished books available via the Internet directly from the author as audio podcasts, usually free

preloaded   audio playback device a hardware device preloaded with a digital audiobook, self-contained (i.e., Playaway)

presence   audio quality that feels authentic, actual—as if you were there

producer   person hired by executive producer; hires talent, books studio time, handles financial details

prosody   vocal melody and tonal inflection

public domain   content not restricted by copyright; audiobooks that may be recorded by volunteers and distributed through LibriVox or an audiobook publisher

punch in, punch and roll   narration edited as recorded, requiring a stop-and-start interruption to the reading as opposed to a continuous record

read-along   an audiobook meant to be listened to while following along with the picture-book text and illustrations

reader engagement   the perception that the narrator was actively involved in the production

repeated sentence (word)   production error in which poor editing results in repeated content

rich recording clarity, clean sound throughout title, not muddy or muted

sequence announcement vocal prompt at end of CD, cassette, or audio portion, also known as tag lines

sibilant distortion or overload of sound resulting in an overemphasis of *s*, *f*, and *ch* sounds

silent intervals silence, such as the space between the chapters

simultaneous release a release date of an audiobook simultaneous with the print book release

sleeve the packaging material that holds printed information or CDs

sound effects establish action, time, place, mood; added audio effects that are referenced in the text or illustrations, often found in read-alongs

sound level overall volume of recording—ideally consistent, not variable or uneven

soundscape the total sound environment, the created audible world of the audiobook

special or bonus features added author interviews or other audio material not found in original text, also known as value-added

spoken word performance an audio presentation that is recording of a seminar, lecture, comedy routine, and so on

straight read narration in the narrator's natural voice

streaming audio digital audiobook playback over a live Internet connection

stress emphasizing a word or syllable—stress on the wrong syllable or wrong word results in changed meaning

studio noise the noise made by clothing, jewelry, page turns, body movements, and other extraneous sound captured in the recording

tag lines comments at beginning or end of audio segment, such as "End of side 2" or "Please insert . . ."

tail end of production

talent person hired to read; may be an actor, author, professional narrator, or celebrity

Talking Book Program audiobook service provided by the National Library Services to the Blind and Physically Handicapped

text-to-speech software   computer program that allows software to create an artificial voice that translates text directly into a digital file

thin   sound quality that strains the ear, difficult to hear

throat   swallows body noise

tinny   sound quality that is artificial, electronic—lacks low frequency

TOC files   table-of-contents files—metadata that ensure that sound files play the audiobook in correct sequence

top   beginning of audiobook

track points (index points)   invisible markings that allow listener to jump to points on audio file—may be of varied length, depending on producer

tummy rumbles   body noise

unabridged   complete, unaltered work

underscore   music under narration

unvoiced   a single narrator performing a straight read in his or her natural voice with no characterization

upcut   choppy edit, noticeable or abrupt editing of sound at the beginning of a word

value-added   extras added to audio title (e.g., visual content, author interview)

vocables   nonword sounds that evoke meaning (e.g., clicks, grunts, sighs)

voice actor   professional narrator

wall of performance   a barrier that may be apparent to a listener who is aware of the voice actor's performance; may be removed by a skilled narrator

widows and orphans   sentences or text fragment split by audio production side, CD, or segment change

woofing the mic   narration causing pops or plosives

word count   used to estimate recording length—typical narrator reads approximately 154 words per minute, or 9,200 words an hour

wrap   the paper with production information that slips in the outer packaging

B

How to Listen

What to Look for When Evaluating an Audiobook

SHARON GROVER

Is the book or story one that lends itself to being read aloud?

- Strong narrative pull often makes for the best listening experience.

How is it narrated?

- Pacing and inflection are critical components of a successful audiobook.
- One reader:

    Fully voiced: the narrator develops a distinct voice for each character.

    Partially voiced: the narrator develops a distinct voice for some characters but differentiates others through pacing and inflection.

    Unvoiced: all characters are differentiated through pacing and inflection.

- More than one reader:

    Male and female readers take gender roles.

    An older voice and a younger voice are used to indicate age differences.

    Full cast (with or without a narrator for the in-between parts).

Read by the actor or by the author?

- Authors can sometimes be great narrators because they are most intimately acquainted with their books.

- But they are, for the most part, untrained readers and may lessen the impact of the story by breathing and/or pausing in the wrong places or through an inability to take on appropriate pacing and inflection.
- Stories about specific cultures are usually best served by a narrator from that culture, which provides an increased measure of authenticity.

Fiction or nonfiction:

- Plot-driven narratives or those with highly developed characters are generally good candidates for the audiobook format.
- Nonfiction doesn't always work as well in an audio format because the narrative is often not the strong point of a work of nonfiction.
- Nonfiction is frequently very dependent on the illustrative matter accompanying the text, which you miss in audiobook format.
- Biography is one form of nonfiction that works well in audiobook format because it often unfolds in a highly narrative fashion.

C

Earphone English Turns Ten

Listening Takes Us Farther Than We Had Imagined

FRANCISCA GOLDSMITH

"You can see the lights go on in the eyes of the kids who can understand spoken English. They can now *get* the book." Ten years after we initiated a pilot project with fewer than half a dozen kids in her high school English-language development classes, Heidi Ramirez Weber and I sat over dinner looking back at where Earphone English has been and the number of unexpected, as well as hoped-for, learnings that hundreds of teens in Berkeley, California, have shown us through the decade.

From our collaboration with those first motivated immigrant teens from Pakistan, Lebanon, and Mexico, over lunchtime sessions in a classroom lost to fire during that first year, the experiences English-language learners have had with the Earphone English audiobook program have come to include an established and school-supported club (along with and in membership competition for this diverse high school's other extensive club options, which include La Raza, Meateaters, Best Buddies, and Knitting Club) and an annual six-week module in English-language development, during which nearly seventy-five freshman through senior learners explore reading with their ears as part of the official curriculum.

Francisca Goldsmith is instructional designer and instructor for Infopeople, a statewide Library Services and Technology Act training project for California libraries.

The English-language-learning population in our school is extensively immigrant, although an occasional European student on a semester- or yearlong foreign exchange has taken part in the club. The English-language development (ELD) department functions with just under two hundred kids, whose English-language facility ranges from so minimal as to put them at risk if they become lost and need to ask directions to those who have refined not only informal but also academic English to the point of gaining acceptance at highly competitive American universities. They hail from Mongolia, China, El Salvador, Nigeria, Eritrea, Turkey, Yemen, Pakistan, Mexico, and on rare occasion Japan, Russia, and Serbia and Montenegro. Because of the broad linguistic diversity, English becomes their lingua franca earlier than in schools with more monolingual English learners.

Because Earphone English is a club, its dynamics change—sometimes dramatically and sometimes subtly—year to year as different students take charge and others provide input with degrees of ownership. Meeting weekly, attendance ranges from a typical group of five in one year to a typical group of fifteen or twenty in other years. Some kids join in ninth grade and stay active until graduation, whereas others struggle through less than a year in an American high school before dropping away from the activity and sometimes away from sight. We've had one highly active member murdered (in his own home) and another develop a club website and social media site, as well as create a lasting logo that echoes the school's mascot, a yellow jacket, with the clever added attribution of headphones.

For the first three or four years after the club was established, and just as ELD teacher Nancy Isaksen began to establish her six-week classroom module with audiobooks, we received state funding for materials (e.g., audiobooks and players, batteries, money for the occasional pizza party) that carried with it the requirement that we report standardized test scores in speaking, reading, writing, and listening proficiency in English. From that, we saw empirical indications—unproven by any formal study to date—that listening to audiobooks seems to help English learners who have weaker auditory and reading skills to strengthen them.

One of our original anticipations seems to have been borne out: the audiobook listeners find self-esteem and pleasure in having access to books popular with their native-English-reading peers, which emboldens the English learners to participate more comfortably in the high school's mainstream. Although early on we found that asking teens to view the print work while listening to it could be frustrating and discordant, we also noticed that the kids who listened came to a quick and self-aware understanding of how punctuation works in spoken (and thus written) English.

Among by-product discoveries have been some other truly important insights:

- Earphone English Club gives teens something that is in the present rather than seeming to be part of a great plan that will reward them in the future.
- The club can be a place to share expertise with the building of a Ning, crafts (paper folding and knitting have figured into some meetings), and other skills that fall outside the specifically literary and linguistic.
- An annual trek to the public library for a movie and pizza celebration has demonstrated to library staff that the kids involved in the club have specific tastes in their movie choices, and these don't break along staff's expectations or assumptions. Among surprises have been the intense interest of boys in the group in *Twilight* and the high demand for a Holocaust film in another year.
- Because Heidi was first introduced to *Speak* as an audiobook that several of her students discovered and loved, she placed it in the ninth-grade curriculum back in 2002.
- Nancy is an avid audiobook listener, whereas Heidi is not; Earphone English has encouraged them to discuss books between them in ways they hadn't explored earlier in their collaborations as teachers.
- Student understanding of and commitment to the public library are built often from the ground up and through the club, meetings of which public library staff regularly visit. This experience has made such deep impressions on some that even years after high school graduation, they continue to be avid public library users.

D

Websites of Audiobook Publishers

AudioGo
www.audiobookshelf.com

BBC Audiobooks America, now AudioGo
www.bbcaudiobooksamerica.com/

Blackstone Audiobooks
www.blackstoneaudio.com

Bolinda Audio
www.bolinda.com

Brilliance Audio
www.brillianceaudio.com

Full Cast Audio
www.fullcastaudio.com

Hachette Audio
www.hachettebookgroup.com/publishing_hachette-audio.aspx

HarperCollins Publishers (audiobook imprints)
Caedmon Audio
www.harpercollins.com/imprints/index.aspx?imprintid=518000
Harper Audio
www.harpercollins.com/imprints/index.aspx?imprintid=517989
HarperChildren's Audio
www.harpercollins.com/imprints/index.aspx?imprintid=517999

Listen and Live Audio
www.listenandlive.com

Live Oak Media
www.liveoakmedia.com

Naxos
www.naxos.com/

Oasis Audio
www.oasisaudio.com
Springwater Imprint
www.oasisaudio.com/springwater.php

Peachtree Publishers
http://peachtree-online.com/index.php/books/category/audio

Penguin Group (Viking)
http://us.penguingroup.com

Random House Publishers (audiobook imprints)
Books on Tape
www.booksontape.com
Listening Library
www.randomhouse.com/audio/listeninglibrary
Random House Audio
www.randomhouse.com/audio

Recorded Books
www.recordedbooks.com

Scholastic Audio
www.scholastic.com/scholasticaudio

Simon and Schuster Audio
http://audio.simonandschuster.com

Tantor Media
www.tantor.com/home-library.asp

Weston Woods
http://westonwoods.scholastic.com

Bibliography

Anderson, Richard C., Elfrieda H. Hiebert, Judith A. Scott, Ian G. Wilkinson, with contributions from members of the Commission on Reading, *Becoming a Nation of Readers: The Report of the Commission on Reading.* Washington, D.C.: U.S. Department of Education, 1985.

Baskin, Barbara H., and Karen Harris. "Heard Any Good Books Lately? The Case for Audiobooks in the Secondary Classroom." *Journal of Reading* 38, no. 5 (1995): 372.

Basu, Biman. "The Saga of Audiobooks." *Anil Aggrawal's Internet Journal of Book Reviews* 7, no. 2 (July–December 2008): 1. www.geradts.com/anil/br/.

Beavin, Kristi. "Audiobooks: Hear! Hear!" *Horn Book Magazine*, May–June 1995, 318–323.

———. "Hear! Hear!" *Horn Book Magazine*, January–February 1996, 105–110.

Beck, Isabel L., and Margaret G. McKeown. "Text Talk: Capturing the Benefits of Read-Aloud Experiences for Young Children." *Reading Teacher* 55, no. 1 (2001): 10–21.

Beers, Kylene. "Listen While You Read: Struggling Readers and Audiobooks." *School Library Journal* 44, no. 4 (1998): 30–35.

Bomar, Linda. "iPods as Reading Tools." *Principal* 85, no. 5 (2006): 52–53.

Burkey, Mary. "The Booklist Odyssey Interview: Arnie Cardillo." *Booklist* 104, no. 13 (2008): 79.

———. "Voices in My Head: The Future of Audio Formats." *Book Links* 18, no. 4 (2009): 50–51.

———. "Voices in My Head: Long-Form Listening." *Book Links* 18, no. 6 (2009): 26–27.

———. "Sounds Good to Me: Listening to Audiobooks with a Critical Ear." *Booklist*, June 1 and 15, 2007, 104.

Carr, Jo. "Producing Audiobooks: How Do They Do It?" *Horn Book Magazine*, March–April 1994, 181.

Chen, Shu-Hsien L. "Improving Reading Skills through Audiobooks." *School Library Media Activities Monthly* 21, no. 1 (2004): 22–25.

Claiborne, Ron, and Hanna Siegel. "New Study Shows Boys Lagging behind Girls in Reading." March 17, 2010. http://abcnews.go.com/WN/study-shows-boys-lagging-girls-reading/story?id=10128586&page=1.

Ditlow, Tim. "Behind the Scenes of an Audiobook." *Publisher's Weekly,* May 14, 2001, 38.

Dowell, Jennifer M. "The Alchemy of Children's Audio: Is There a Magic Formula?" *AudioFile Magazine,* April–May 2001, 18–23.

Farrell, Beth. "The Lowdown on Audio Downloads." *Library Journal* 105, no. 9 (2010): 26–29.

Fellerer, Sue. "The Playaway: A Tool to Help Make Reading Fun." *Library Media Connection* 27, no. 6 (2009): 52–53.

Ferreri, Patricia. "Listening for Literacy." *Teaching Pre K–8* 31, no. 2 (2000): 61.

Freeman, Matt. "Sound Choices." *Reading Today* 21, no. 2 (2003): 24.

Goldenberg, Claude. "Teaching English Language Learners: What the Research Does—and Does Not—Say." *American Educator* 32, no. 2 (2008): 8–23, 42–44.

Goldsmith, Francisca. "Earphone English." *School Library Journal* 48, no. 5 (2002): 50–53.

Grover, Sharon, and AudioFile editors. "Audiobooks on the Go: Summer Listening for Kids and Families, Updated 2011 Edition." *AudioFile Magazine,* April–May 2011, 23–27. http://www.audiofilemagazine.com/abotg11.html.

Grover, Sharon, and Lizette Hannegan. "Hear and Now: Connecting Outstanding Audiobooks to Library and Classroom Instruction." *Teacher Librarian* 35, no. 3 (2008): 17–21.

———. "Not Just for Listening: Integrating Audiobooks into the Curriculum." *Book Links* 14, no. 5 (2005): 16–19.

Harris, Karen. "Stellar Science Audiobooks." *Book Links* 11, no. 2 (2001): 30–31.

Hipple, Ted. "Horizons: Audiobooks in the Classroom." *AudioFile Magazine,* June 1996, 6–7.

Holley, Pam Spencer. "The Booklist Odyssey Interview: Troy Juliar." *Booklist* 105, no. 4 (2009): 72.

"How to Increase Reading Skills through Recorded Books." *NEA Today* 19, no. 5 (2001): 27.

Jemtegaard, Kristi. "The Booklist Interview: Tim Ditlow." *Booklist* 101, no. 22 (2005): 2048.

———. "Readers vs. Listeners." *Booklist* 101, no. 5 (2005): 1399.

Kempf, Erika L. "When Author Is Narrator: Audiobooks Read by the Author." *Book Links* 12, no. 6 (2003): 32–36.

Koskinen, Patricia, Irene H. Blum, Nancy Tennant, E. Marie Parker, Mary Straub, and Christine Curry. "Have You Heard Any Good Books Lately? Encouraging Shared Reading at Home with Books and Audiotapes." Instructional Resource No. 15 (1995) 31 pp. (ED385827).

Kresh, Paul. "Readers Worthy of the Books They're Reading." *New York Times,* July 2, 1989, p. 22.

Larson, Jeanette. "Listen Up! What's New in Audiobooks." *Library Media Connection* 29, no. 4 (2011): 44–45.

———. "Listen Up! What's New in Audiobooks." *Library Media Connection* 26, no. 4 (2008): 44–45.

Lesesne, Teri. "Why Listen at All?" *VOYA,* August 2007, 221.

Locke, Deborah. "The Audio Time Machine." *Book Links* 11, no. 6 (2002): 14.

———. "Heard Any Good Books Lately?" *Book Links* 11, no. 2 (2001): 26–28.

Mandell, Phyllis Levy. "Heard Any Good Books Lately?" *School Library Journal* 56, no. 8 (2010): 32–38.

Marchionda, Denise. "A Bridge to Literacy: Creating Lifelong Readers through Audiobooks." *AudioFile Magazine,* August–September 2001, pp. 19–20, 55.

Marchionda, Denise L. "Listening to Learn English." *AudioFile Magazine,* April–May 2002, p. 20–23.

Maughan, Shannon. "Audiobooks 2.0." *Publisher's Weekly,* May 10, 2010, 11–16.

———. "Coville's Full Cast Audio." *Publisher's Weekly,* May 6, 2002, 20.

———. "Sounds Like Celebration." *Publisher's Weekly,* March 7, 2005, 24–25.

———. "Summer Listening 101." *Publisher's Weekly,* June 14, 2004, 37.

McCormick, Myra. "Harry Potter to Cast a Spell over Audio." *Billboard,* October 9, 1999, 77.

McPherson, Keith. "Listening Carefully." *Teacher Librarian* 35, no. 4 (2008): 73–75.

Miller, Laura. "*War and Peace* Made Easy." *Salon,* June 30, 2010. www.salon.com/books/laura_miller/2010/06/30/audiobooks.

Milliot, Jim. "Profiling Audiobook Customers." *Publisher's Weekly,* November 29, 2010, 4.

Myrick, Ellen. "Say It with Music: Audiobooks with Pizzazz." *Booklist* 105, no. 5 (2008): 64.

Noland, Liz. "Why Listening Is Good for *All* Kids—Especially in the Digital Age." *AudioFile Magazine,* April–May 2011, 13–15.

Saricks, Joyce. "At Leisure: Rediscovering the Classics—Through Audiobooks." *Booklist* 106, nos. 19–20 (2010): 29.

Schnol, Janet. "The Making of a Children's Audiotape: Poet Jack Prelutsky Goes into the Recording Studio." *Publisher's Weekly*, September 20, 1991, 46.

Smith, Shawnee. "Listening Library Outlasts Competition." *Billboard*, September 6, 1997, 85.

Varley, Pamela. "As Good as Reading? Kids and the Audiobook Revolution." *Horn Book Magazine*, May–June 2002, 251–262.

Von Drasek, Lisa. "Heard Any Good Books Lately?" *Teaching Pre K–8* 34, no. 8 (2004): 90–91.

Wilde, Susie, and Jeanette Larson. "Listen! It's Good for Kids." *AudioFile Magazine*, April–May 2007, 22–25.

Wolfson, Gene. "Using Audiobooks to Meet the Needs of Adolescent Readers." *American Secondary Education* 36, no. 2 (2008): 105–117.

Wysocki, Barbara. "Louder, Please. For Some Kids, the Best Way to Read Is to Turn Up the Volume." *School Library Journal* 51, no. 4 (2005): 510.

Yokota, Junko, and Miriam Martinez. "Authentic Listening Experiences: Multicultural Audiobooks." *Book Links* 13, no. 3 (2004): 30.

Index